# Tips

- Keep your child's supplies in a container so that everything is close at hand.
- Explain directions before your child begins a new type of activity.
- Show your child how the illustrations help show what to do.
- Encourage your child to pick up and throw away all scraps when a project is finished.

# Supplies

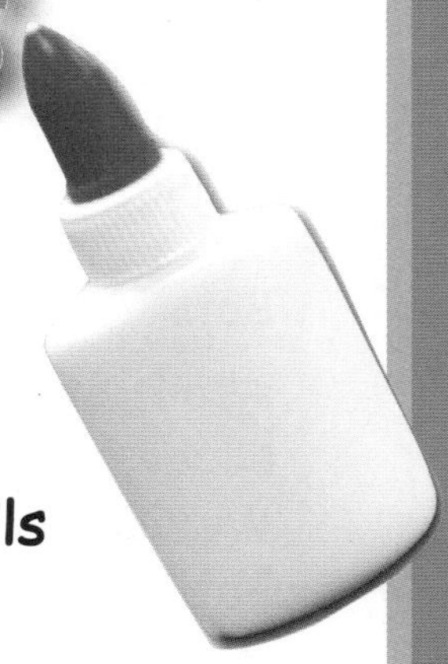

- scissors
- glue stick or glue
- crayons or colored pencils
- marking pens
- pencil
- clear tape
- some projects may require additional supplies

# Table of Contents

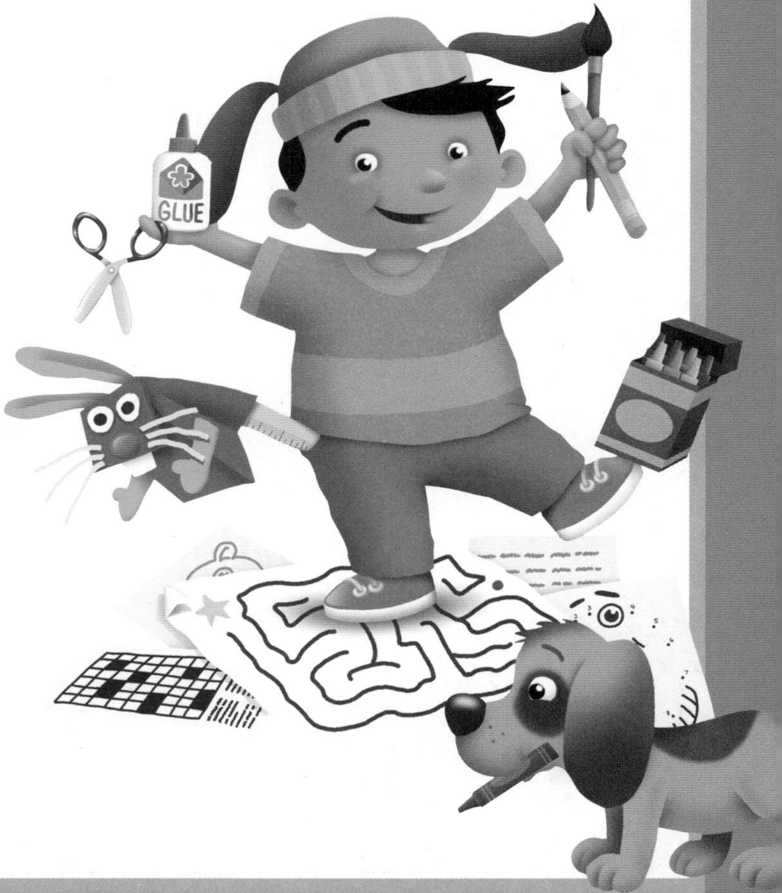
GLUE

# PLAY BALL!

Find the names of all the ball games.

| | | | | | | | | | | | | |
|---|---|---|---|---|---|---|---|---|---|---|---|---|
| B | A | S | K | E | T | B | A | L | L | F | V | B |
| N | O | B | A | S | E | B | A | L | L | O | O | A |
| R | U | G | B | Y | N | G | O | U | T | O | L | D |
| B | H | D | B | I | N | T | O | N | R | T | L | M |
| O | O | S | A | P | I | N | P | L | E | B | E | I |
| W | C | O | L | W | S | I | N | O | F | A | Y | N |
| L | K | C | R | I | C | K | E | T | O | L | B | T |
| I | E | C | B | A | L | L | B | A | L | L | A | O |
| N | Y | E | F | C | R | O | Q | U | E | T | L | N |
| G | N | R | P | I | N | G | P | O | N | G | L | Q |

## Word Box

| | | | | |
|---|---|---|---|---|
| badminton | croquet | pool | baseball | cricket |
| football | rugby | basketball | golf | ping-pong |
| soccer | bowling | hockey | tennis | volleyball |

# LOST BALLS

Coach is unhappy. All of the balls are lost.
See how many you can find. Color them.

7
2
11
5
20
6
4
10
3
17
8

# SAL, THE SOCCER STAR

Sal runs out the door
and races down the street.
He kicks his soccer ball
with his busy feet.

He hits it with his head,
then dribbles it far,
dreaming of the day
he'll be a soccer star!

List three ways Sal moves the soccer ball.

1. ______________________________

2. ______________________________

3. ______________________________

# FOOTBALL PLAYER

Draw and color the other side of the football player.

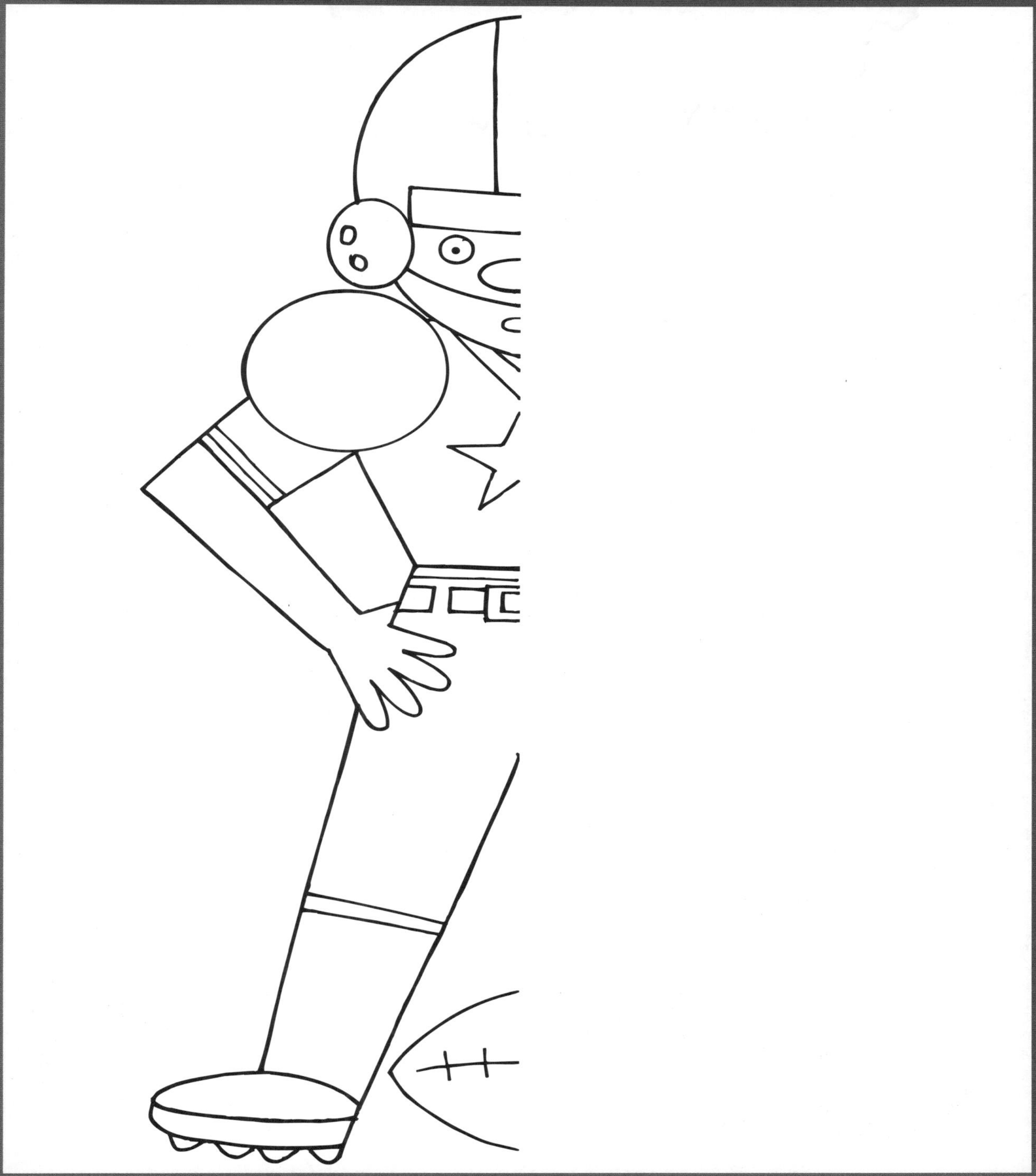

# WHAT IS IT?

Start at 5. Count by 5s to connect the dots.

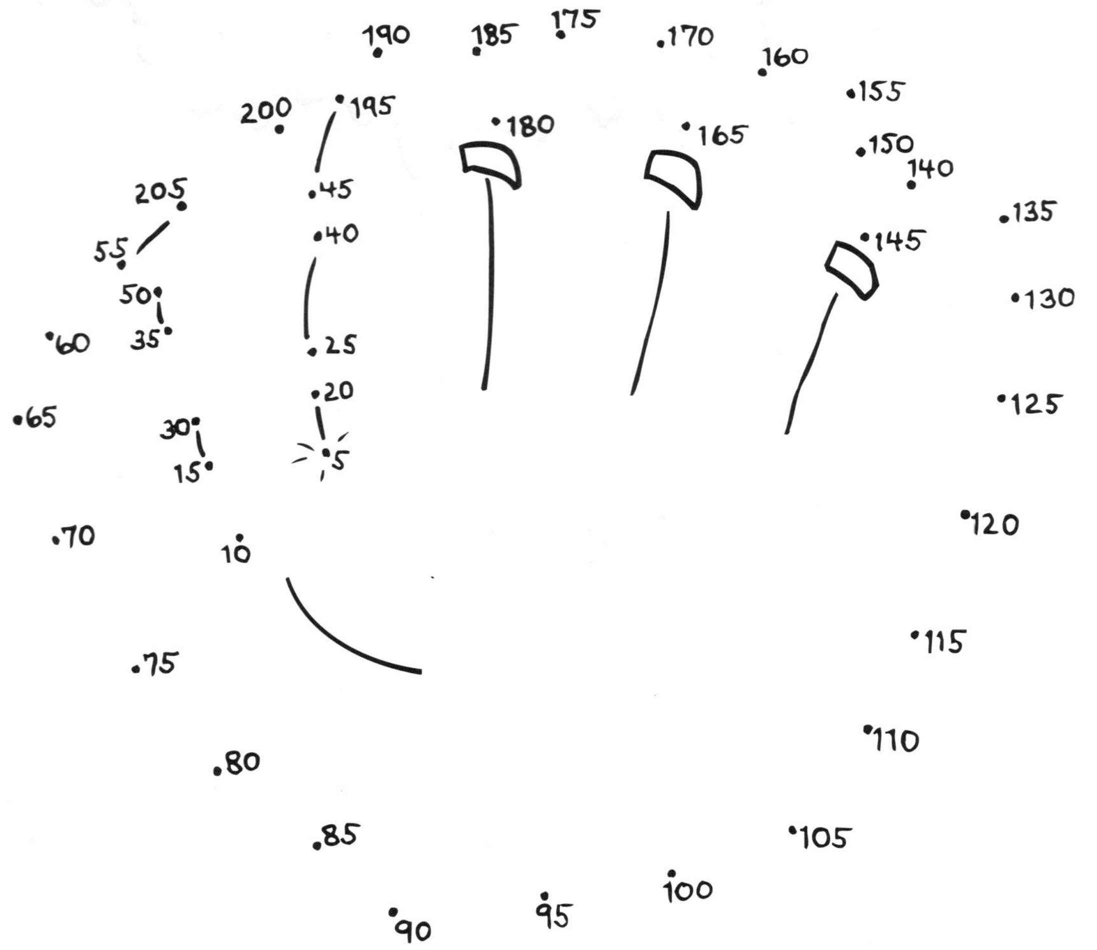

5
10
15
20
25
30
35
40
45
50
55
60
65
70
75
80
85
90
95
100
105
110
115
120
125
130
135
140
145
150
155
160
165
170
175
180
185
190
195
200
205


Circle the ball you would use with the mystery picture.

# BALL GAMES

Use the clues to solve the crossword puzzle.

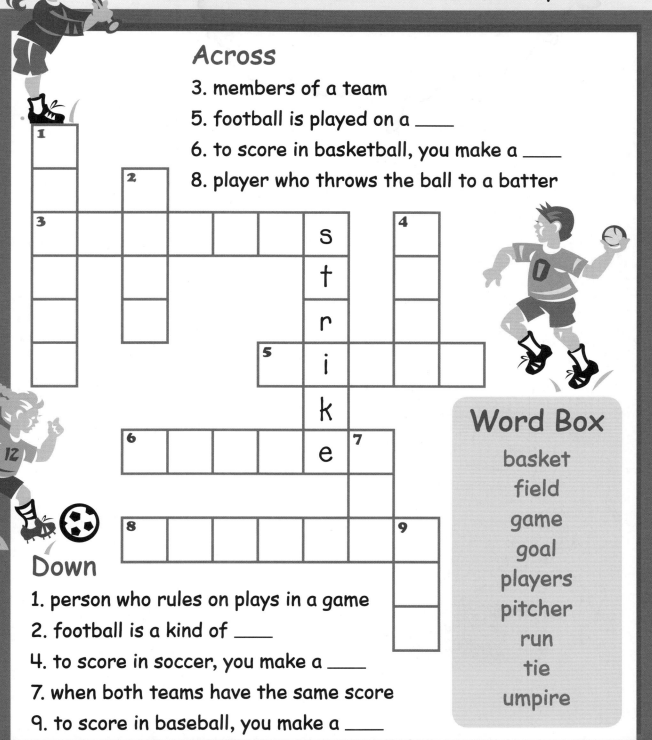

## Across

3. members of a team
5. football is played on a ____
6. to score in basketball, you make a ____
8. player who throws the ball to a batter

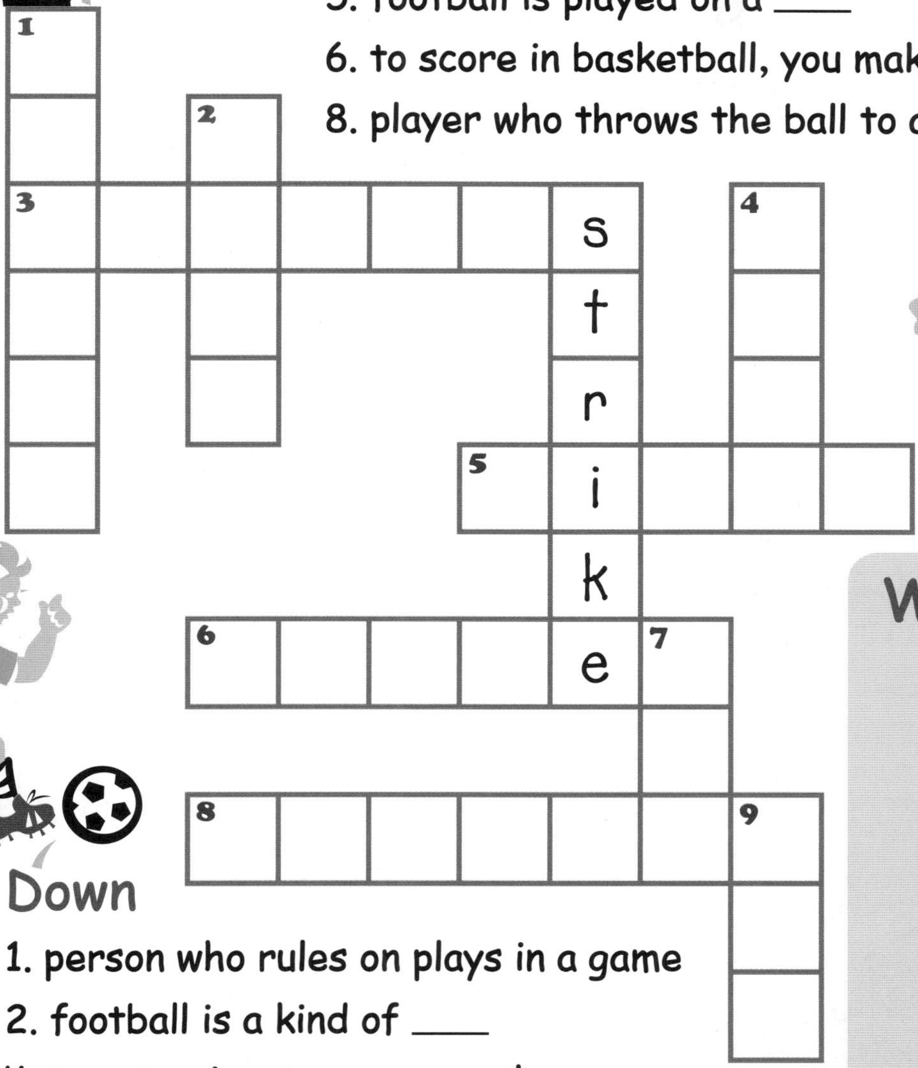
1
2
3
4
5
6
7
8
9
s
t
r
i
k
e

## Down

1. person who rules on plays in a game
2. football is a kind of ____
4. to score in soccer, you make a ____
7. when both teams have the same score
9. to score in baseball, you make a ____

### Word Box

basket
field
game
goal
players
pitcher
run
tie
umpire

# GO FOR A GOAL

Help the soccer player make a goal.

SCORE

# Tomato Soup

Draw and color the other side.

I like tomato soup. **yes** **no**

# The Magic Pot

A mother and her son sat by their hut. They felt as empty as hollow logs. They worked hard. But they did not have enough food to keep their stomachs full.

One day, the boy met a funny little man. The man saw that the boy was hungry. He felt sorry for the boy and gave him a magic pot. The man showed the boy how to use the pot. When the pot heard the words "Cook, Magic Pot, cook!" it filled itself with tasty soup. When it heard "Stop, Magic Pot, stop!" it stopped.

The boy took the pot home. He made tasty soup for his mother. They ate and ate. They were as full as sausages stuffed for market. Each day, the boy and his mother worked hard. Then they ate the tasty soup the boy made with the magic pot.

One day, the boy took a load of wood to town to sell. While he was gone, his mother got hungry. She had watched her son cook soup with the magic pot. She put the pot in the middle of the table. She said, "Cook, Magic Pot, cook!"

The magic pot bubbled. It filled with tasty soup. The woman ate and ate and ate. The magic pot kept bubbling. The woman did not remember the words to make the pot stop.

The soup spilled over the edge of the pot. The pot kept bubbling. The soup spilled off the table. The pot kept bubbling. The soup spilled out the door. Soon, soup was running down the road.

On his way home from town, the boy saw a river of soup running down the road. He jumped out of the way. He ran into his house. He yelled, "Stop, Magic Pot, stop!"

The pot stopped. The last of the soup ran out the door. From that day on, the boy carried his pot with him whenever he went out. His mother never again tried to use magic that she didn't understand.

# Runaway Soup

Draw a line from the boy to the Magic Pot.

# My Magic Pot

Count by 2s to connect the dots. Draw what is in your magic pot.

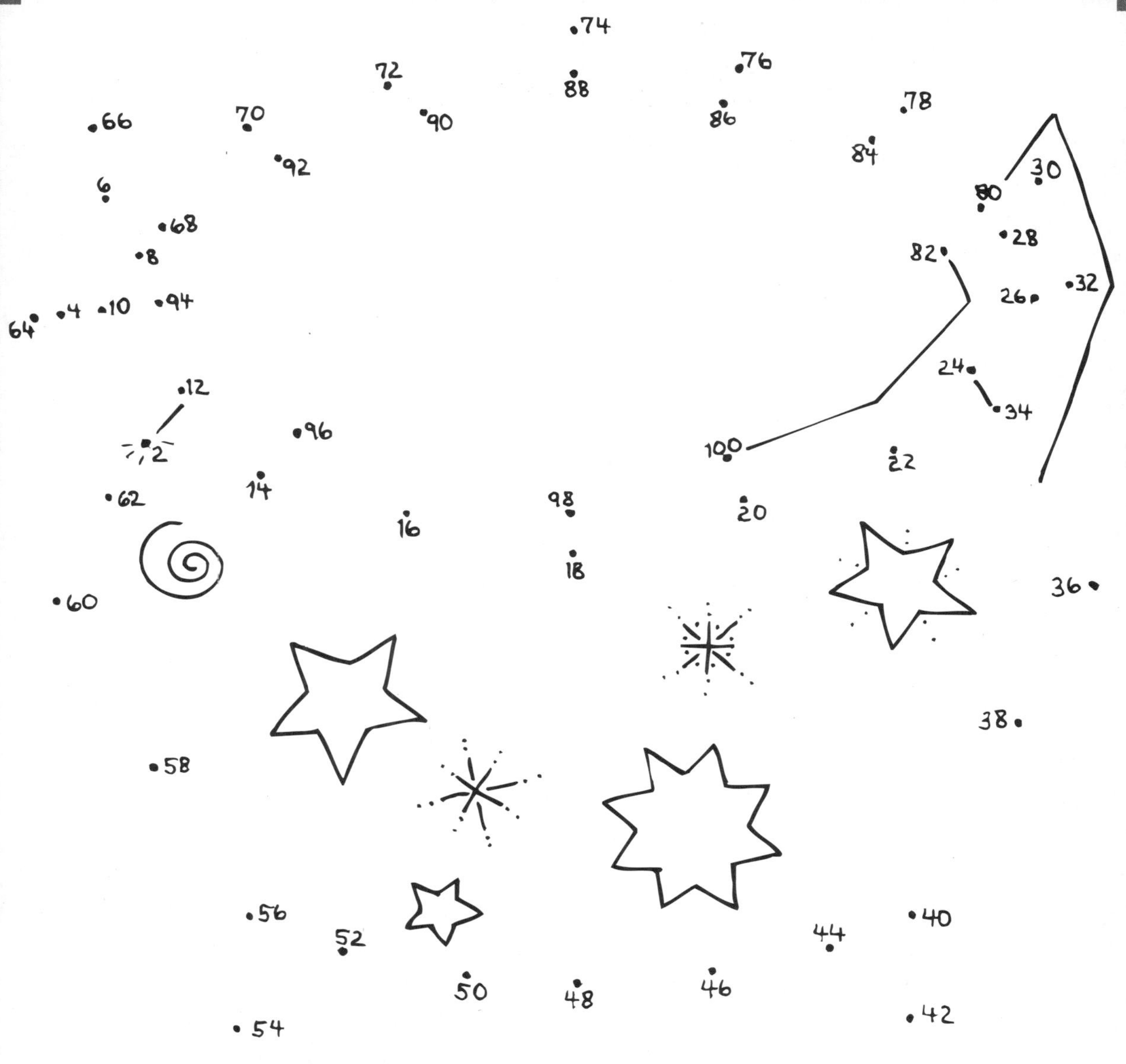

74
72
88
76
70
90
86
78
66
92
84
6
80
30
68
28
8
82
26
32
64
4
10
94
24
12
34
96
2
100
22
14
62
98
20
16
18
36
60
38
58
56
52
44
40
50
48
46
42
54


What kind of magic pot would you like to have? Tell why.

# Vegetable Soup

Find the vegetables in the soup pot.

| | | | | | | | | | | |
|---|---|---|---|---|---|---|---|---|---|---|
| P | O | T | A | T | O | E | S | C | O | G |
| A | E | Y | X | S | U | L | T | A | B | A |
| R | C | A | A | C | E | L | E | R | Y | R |
| S | A | T | S | M | P | O | T | R | B | L |
| N | R | O | N | I | O | N | O | O | E | I |
| I | T | U | R | N | I | P | P | T | A | C |
| P | S | P | I | N | A | C | H | C | N | I |
| R | U | T | A | B | A | G | A | Z | S | N |

## Word Box

| | | | |
|---|---|---|---|
| beans | garlic | peas | spinach |
| carrot | onion | potatoes | turnip |
| celery | parsnip | rutabaga | yam |

# Soup Sale

Mrs. G bought 5 cans of soup on sale. The cans were on sale because they did not have labels. Mrs. G needs your help to find out what kind of soup is in each can.

Read all the clues below. Use them to name the soup in each can. Write the number of each kind of soup on the cans.

- The first and last cans are the same kind of soup.
- Pea soup is in the middle can.
- Tomato soup is on the right side of the pea soup.
- Vegetable soup is in the first can.
- Carrot soup is between the vegetable soup and the pea soup.

1
Carrot
2
Pea
3
Tomato
4
Vegetable

# A Limerick

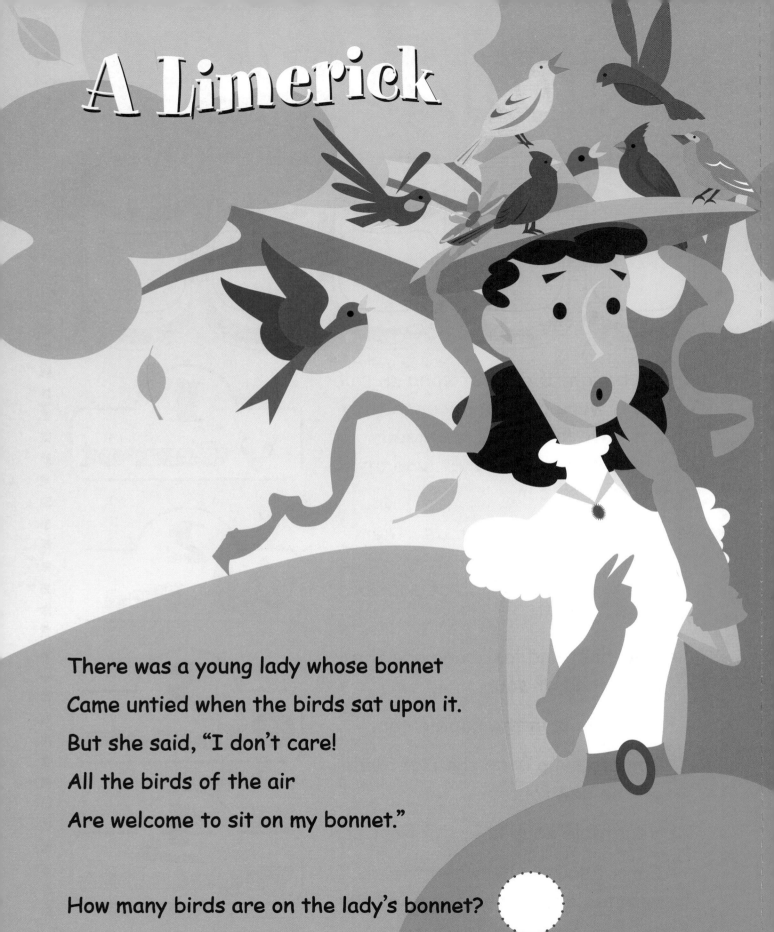

There was a young lady whose bonnet
Came untied when the birds sat upon it.
But she said, "I don't care!
All the birds of the air
Are welcome to sit on my bonnet."

How many birds are on the lady's bonnet?

# Birds of the Air

Find the birds in the word search.

| | | | | | | | | | | | |
|---|---|---|---|---|---|---|---|---|---|---|---|
| R | C | A | R | D | I | N | A | L | C | N | Z |
| M | O | C | K | I | N | G | B | I | R | D | V |
| D | A | B | H | E | L | P | L | O | O | K | U |
| D | U | N | I | A | X | C | U | B | W | E | L |
| C | O | C | A | N | W | Z | E | B | R | A | T |
| O | X | V | K | I | C | K | J | C | A | T | U |
| W | W | R | E | N | Z | E | A | G | L | E | R |
| P | E | L | I | C | A | N | Y | D | O | G | E |
| H | U | M | M | I | N | G | B | I | R | D | X |

## Word Box

| | | | |
|---|---|---|---|
| blue jay | dove | hummingbird | robin |
| cardinal | eagle | mockingbird | vulture |
| crow | hawk | pelican | wren |

# Flock of Birds

Two birds in this flock are exactly the same.
Find the two birds and draw a circle around them.

# About Bats

Cut out the story. Staple the pages together in order.

staple

## A Bat's Body

staple

A bat has wings instead of arms.
The wings are made of muscle, bones,
and skin. Strong muscles flap the wings.

1

A bat has curved claws on its feet.
The claws help the bat to hang upside
down. It won't fall even when it is asleep.

3

A bat uses its tail for balance and for making turns. Some bats use their tails to help them stop.

2

A bat has a furry body.
Bats come in many colors.
Some even have stripes or spots.
It helps the bat blend in with its surroundings.

4

# Name the Parts

**Word Box**

body
claw
ear
eye
foot
head
leg
mouth
nose
tail
thumb
wing

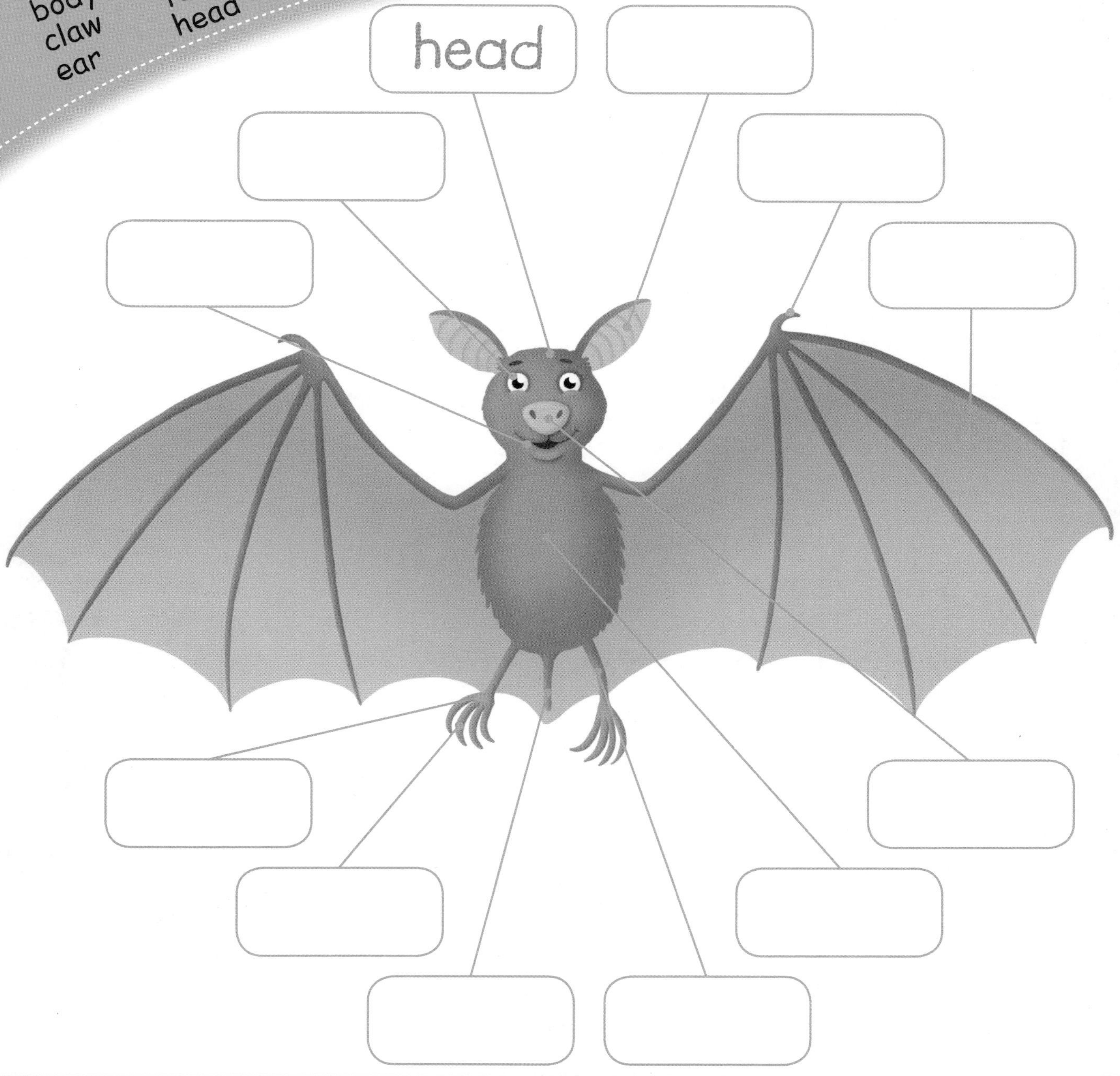
head

# We Can Fly

Read about bats and birds.

A bat is a mammal.

A bat has fur, or hair.

A baby bat is born live.

A baby bat drinks milk from its mother's body.

A bat has wings.

A bat can fly.

A bird has feathers.

A baby bird hatches from an egg.

A baby bird is fed food from its mother's mouth.

A bird has wings.

A bird can fly.

# Bat, Bird, or Both?

Make an **X** in the box if it is true.

bat
bird


| | bat | bird |
|---|---|---|
| 1. I have fur. | ☐ | ☐ |
| 2. I have feathers. | ☐ | ☐ |
| 3. I have wings. | ☐ | ☐ |
| 4. I lay eggs. | ☐ | ☐ |
| 5. I feed milk to my babies. | ☐ | ☐ |
| 6. I can fly. | ☐ | ☐ |

How are birds and bats alike?

______________________________

______________________________

______________________________

# A Flying Fox

A flying fox is a large bat that eats fruit.
Draw and color the other side of this fruit bat.

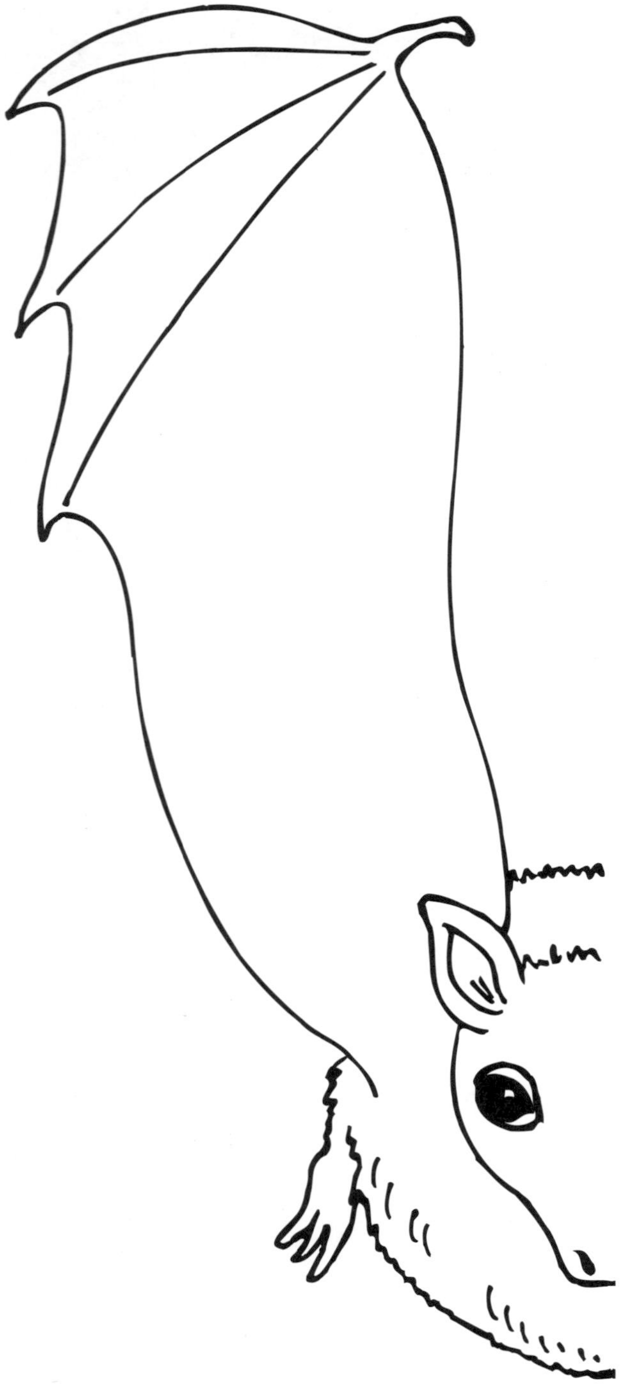

# Who Am I?

Use the code to name each bat.

| | a | b | c | d | e |
|---|---|---|---|---|---|
| 1 | A | B | E | F | G |
| 2 | I | L | M | N | O |
| 3 | P | R | T | U | V |
| 4 | X | Y | | | |

I am the largest bat. I have a wingspan of 6 feet.
Who am I?

___ ___ ___ ___ ___ ___
1d 2b 4b 2a 2d 1e

___ ___ ___
1d 2e 4a

I am the smallest bat. I weigh less than a penny.
Who am I?

___ ___ ___ ___ ___ ___ ___ ___ ___
1b 3d 2c 1b 2b 1c 1b 1c 1c

___ ___ ___
1b 1a 3c

I am a bat that eats blood. Who am I?

___ ___ ___ ___ ___ ___ ___
3e 1a 2c 3a 2a 3b 1c

___ ___ ___
1b 1a 3c

# Hungry Bat

This bat flies around catching insects to eat. Count by 2s to connect the dots. Then draw some tasty insects for the bat to eat.

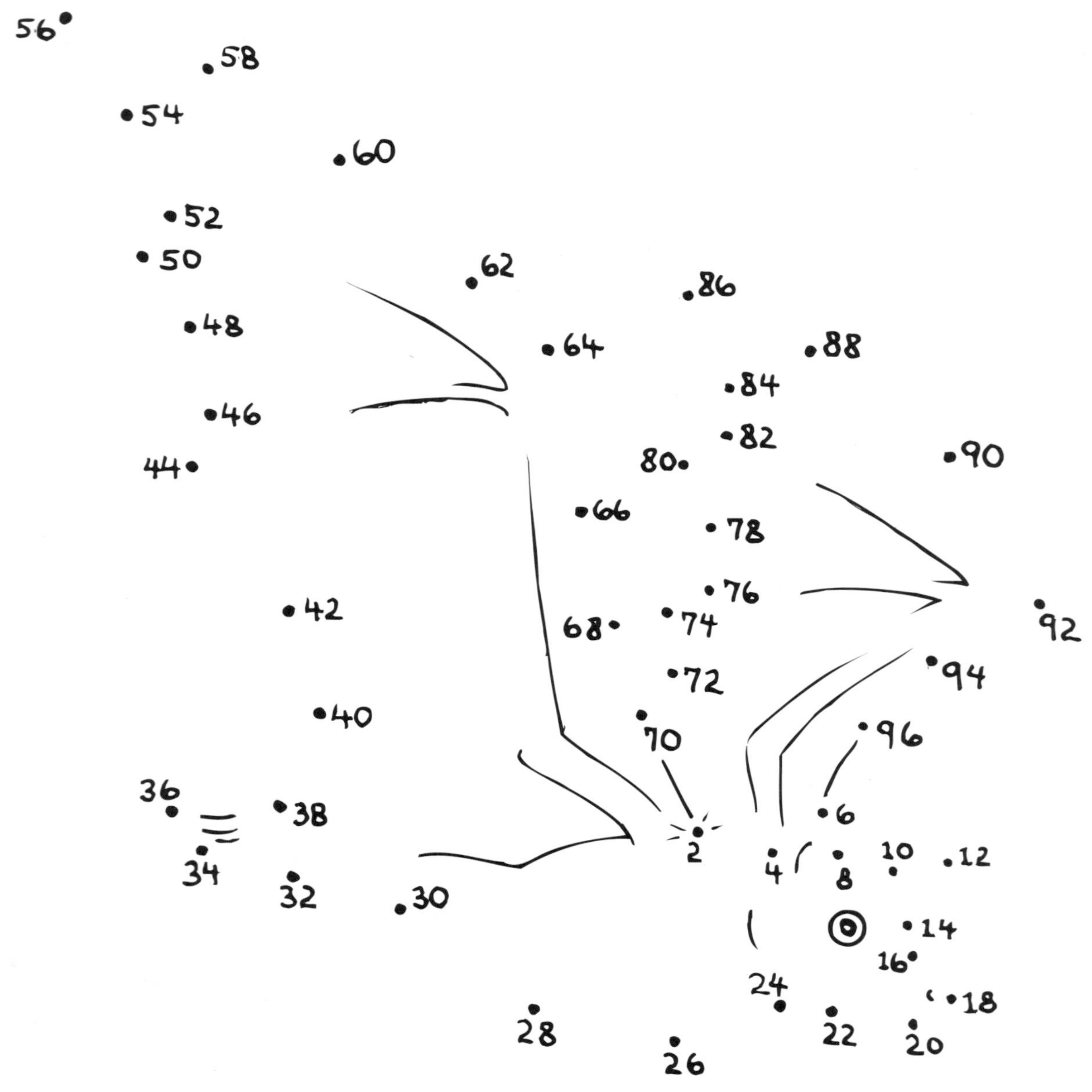

2
4
6
8
10
12
14
16
18
20
22
24
26
28
30
32
34
36
38
40
42
44
46
48
50
52
54
56
58
60
62
64
66
68
70
72
74
76
78
80
82
84
86
88
90
92
94
96

# Night Hunter

Draw a line to guide the bat out of its cave.

EXIT

# Bat Mobile

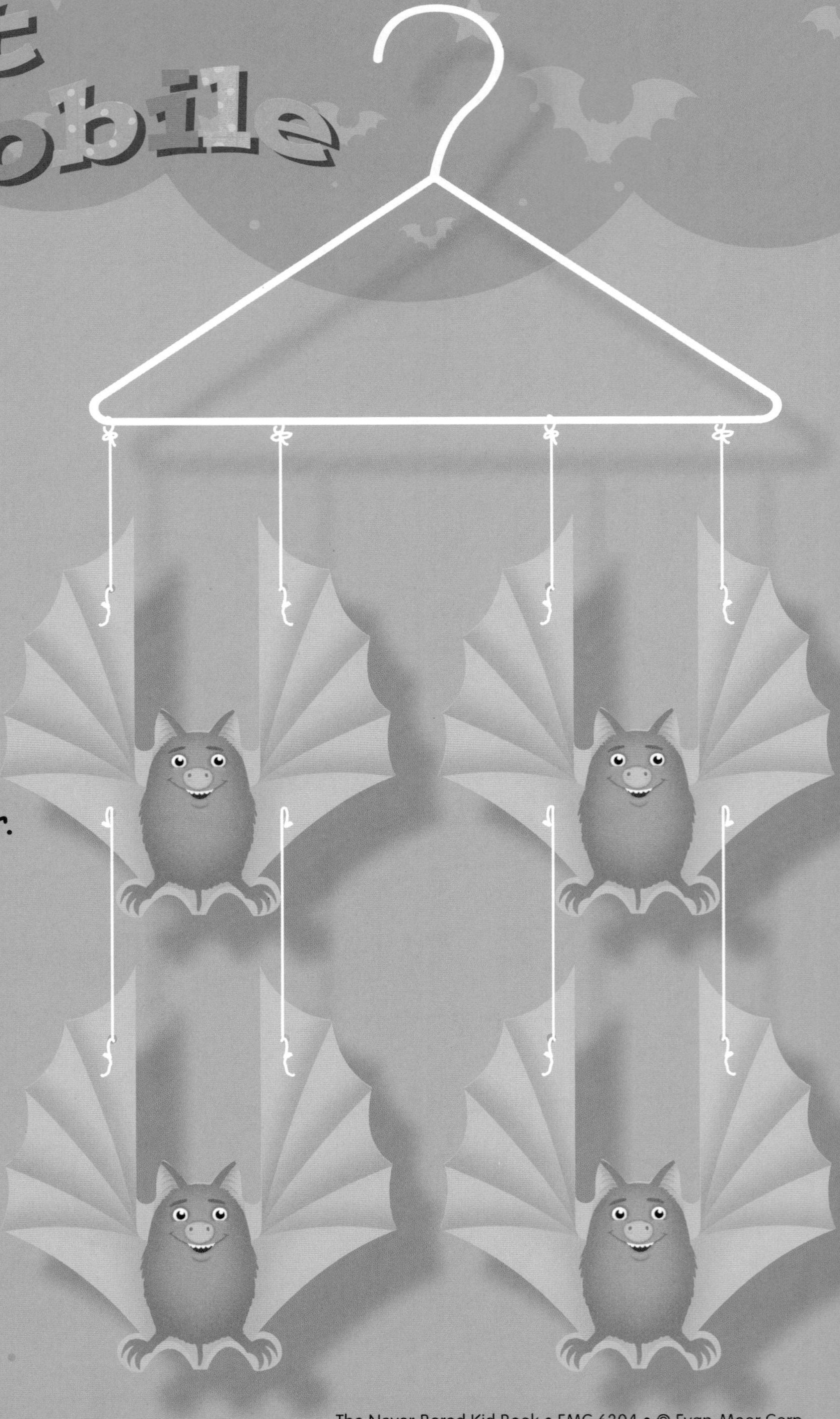

1. Cut out the bat patterns.

2. Punch the holes as marked.

3. Use string to tie the bats to the hanger and to each other.

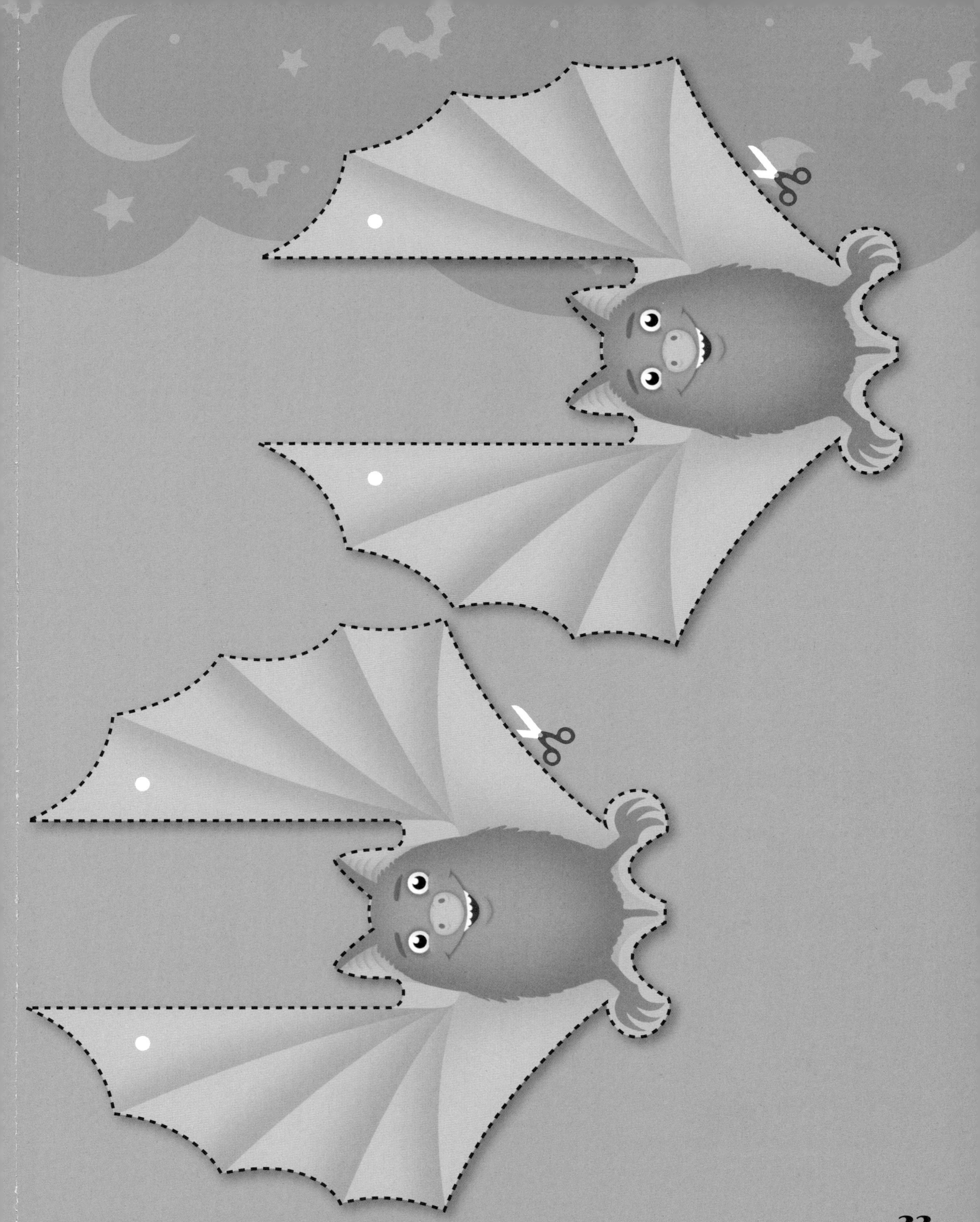

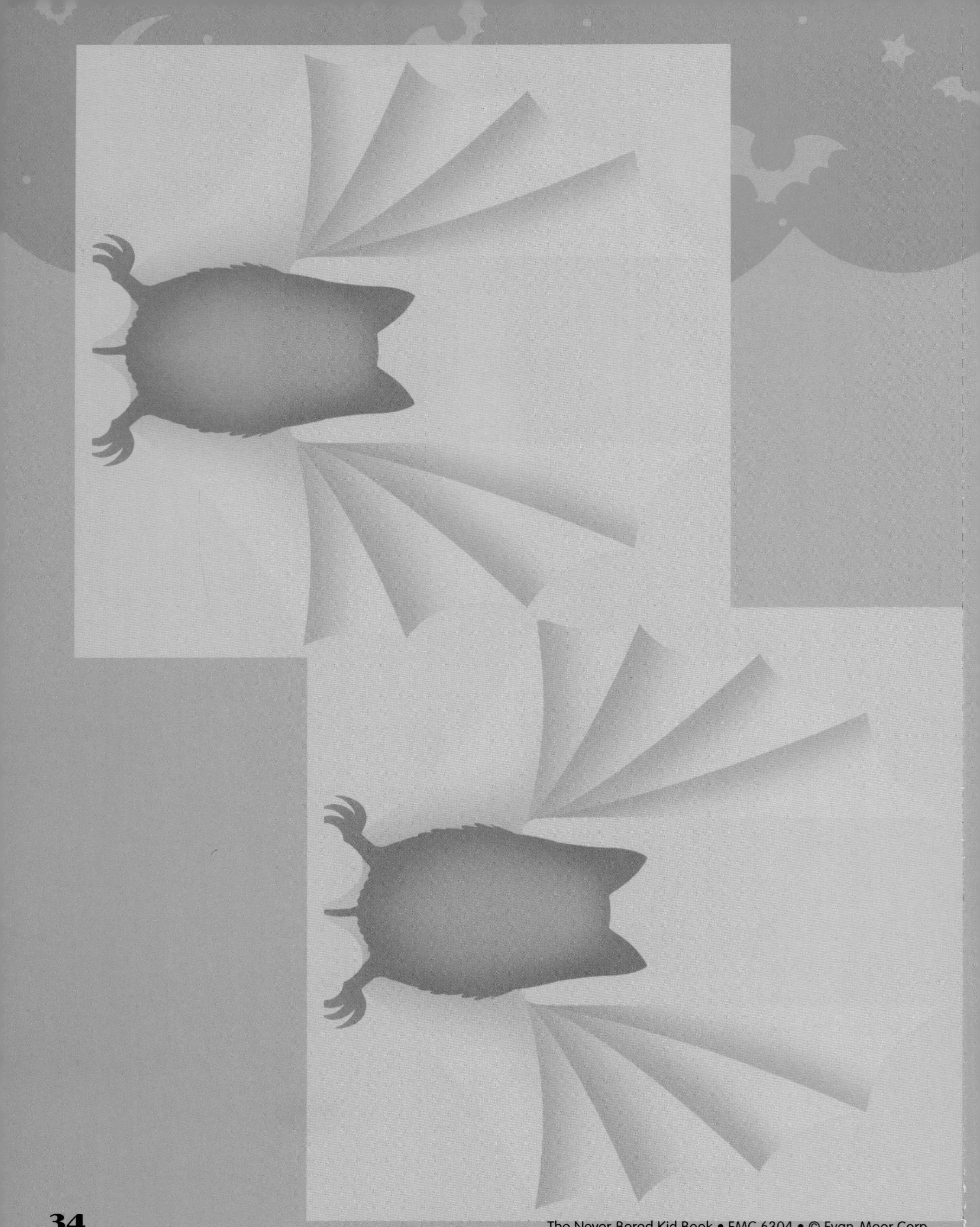

# Race Car Puzzle

**Cut out the pieces. Glue them onto page 37.**

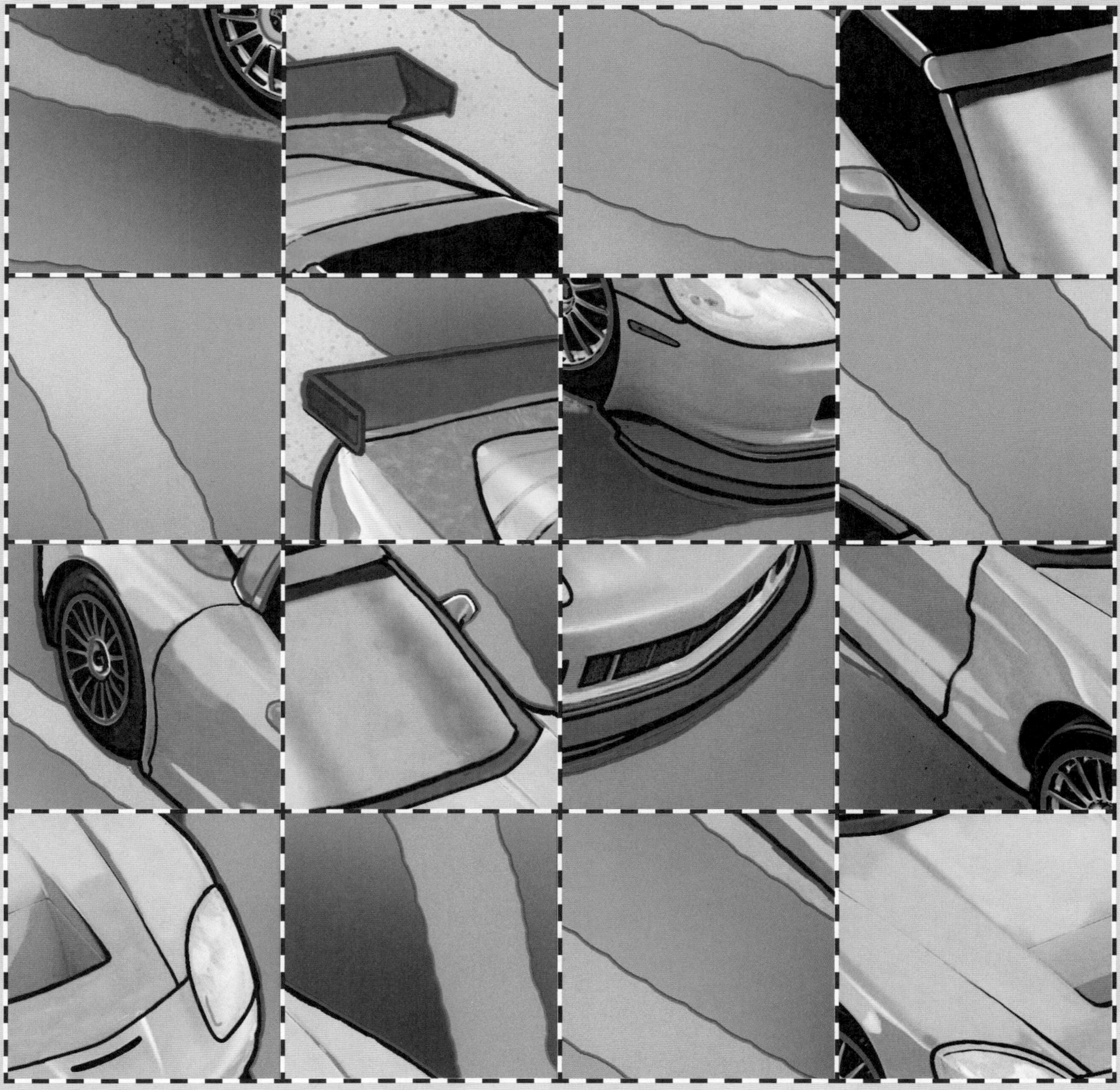

# At the Races

| | | | |
|---|---|---|---|
| glue | glue | glue | glue |
| glue | glue | glue | glue |
| glue | glue | glue | glue |
| glue | glue | glue | glue |

# A Race Car

Draw the race car.
Color it your
favorite color.

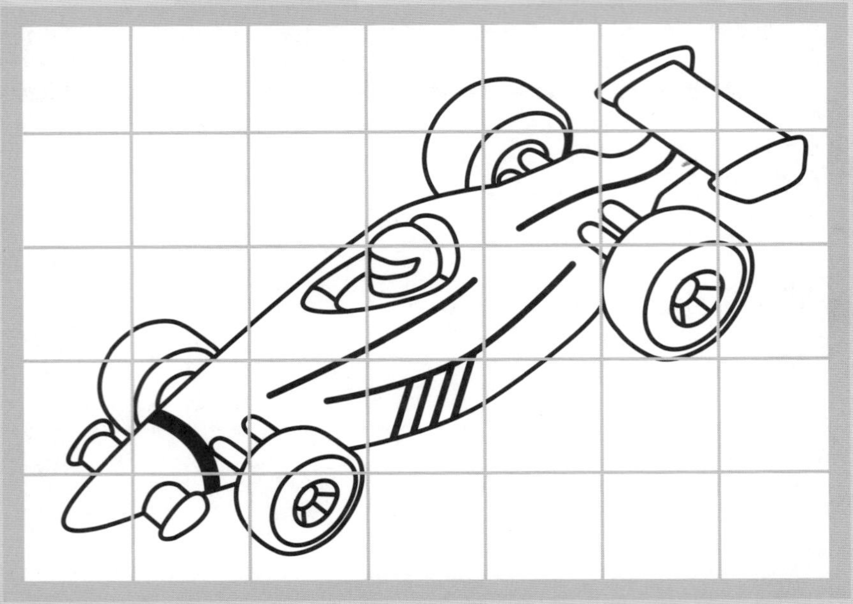

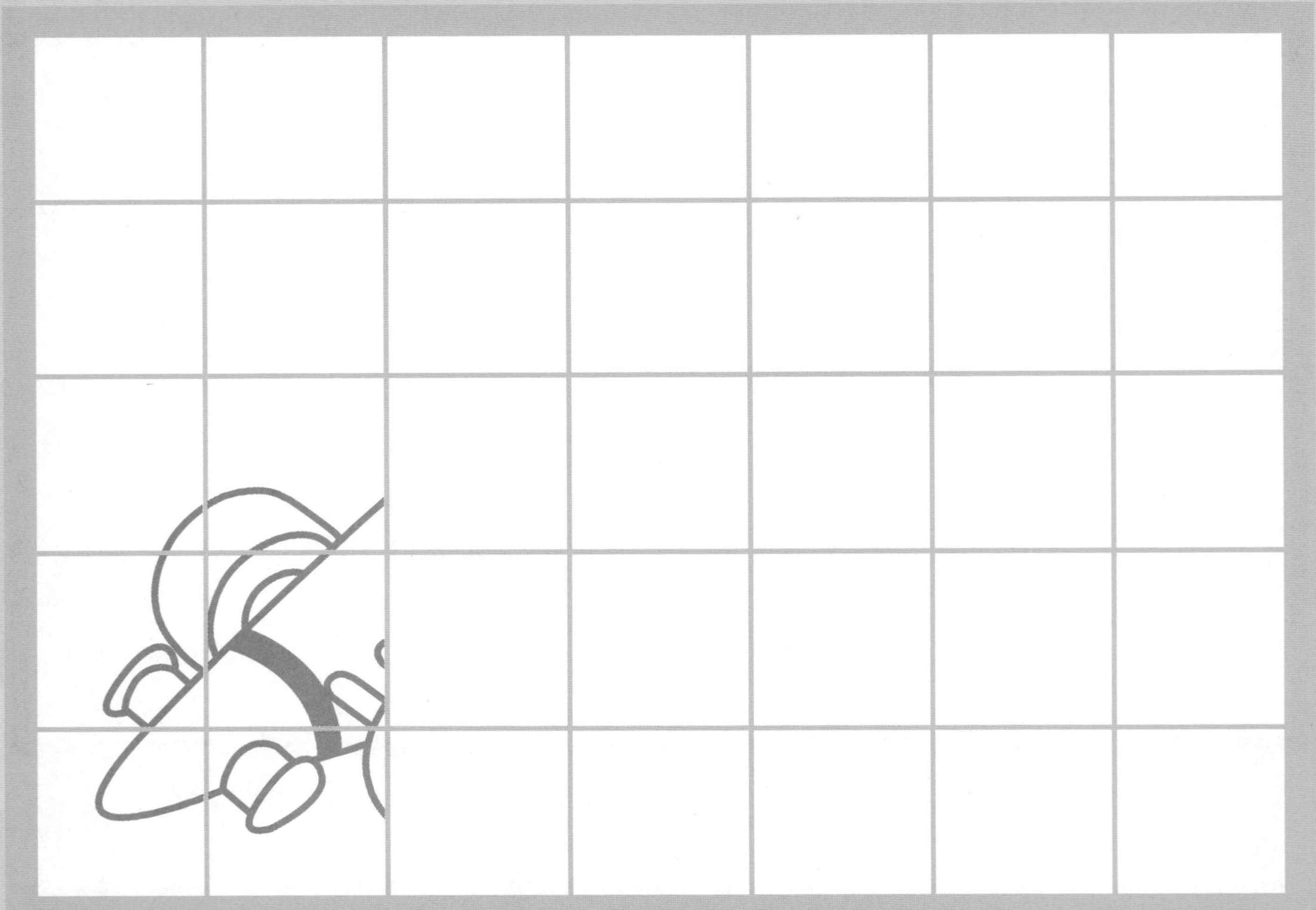

# Around the Race Track

Circle what is wrong in this picture.

1
2
GO
3


What do you think is the funniest mistake in the picture?

# Color by 5s

Count by 5s. Find the numbers you write. Color the sections the numbers are in.

5 10 ___ ___ ___ ___ ___ ___ ___ ___

___ ___ ___ ___ ___ ___ ___ ___ ___ ___

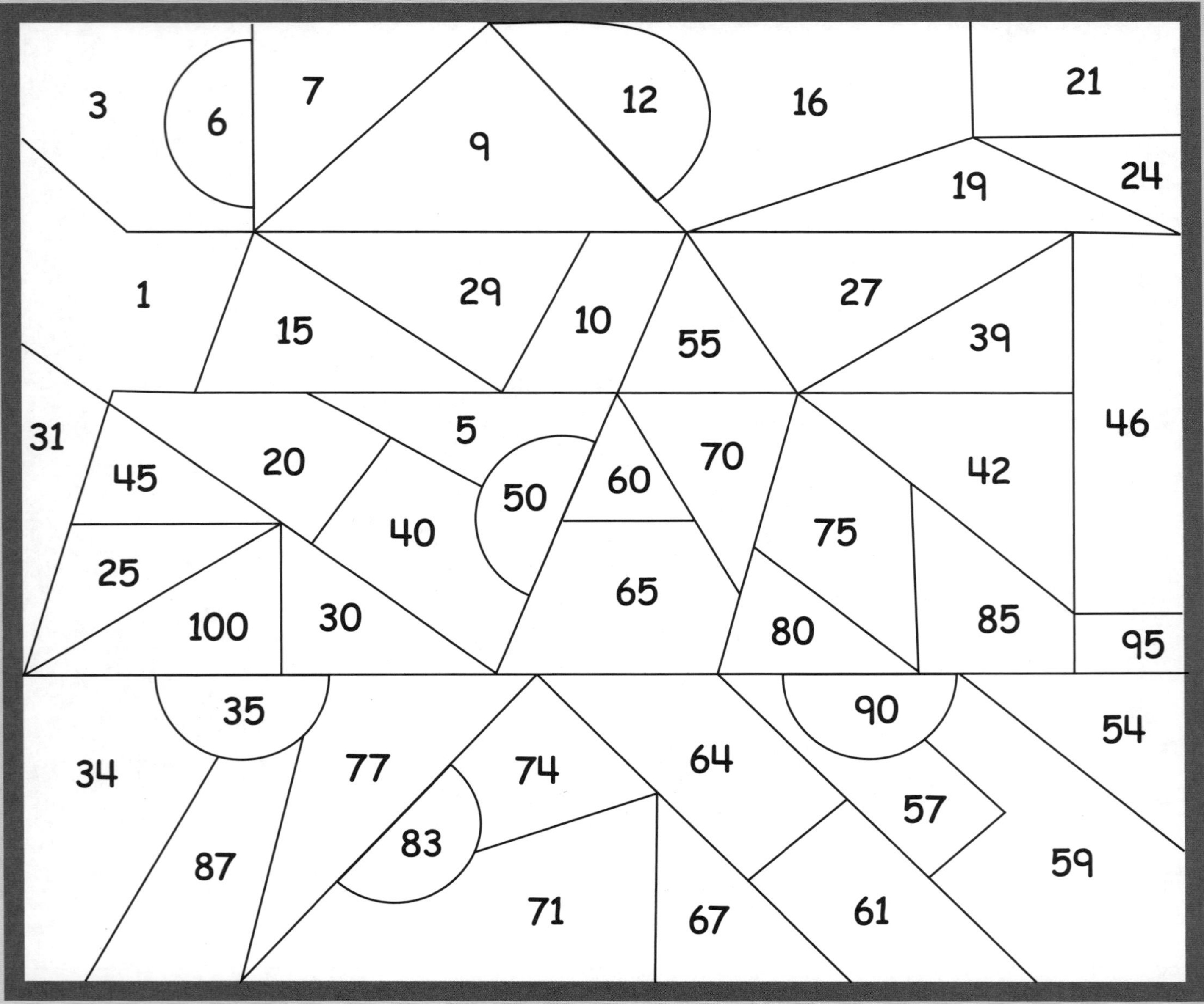

3
6
7
9
12
16
21
19
24
1
15
29
10
55
27
39
31
45
20
5
50
60
70
42
46
25
40
75
100
30
65
80
85
95
35
90
54
34
77
74
64
57
83
87
71
67
61
59


My race car is number

# Voyage in Space

1. Cut out the story pages.
2. Cut out the spaceship, circles, triangles, hexagons, and squares on page 45.
3. On pages 2, 3, 4, and 5 you have a choice to make. Glue your choice on the correct page.
4. Staple the pages together in order.
5. Write about your voyage in space.
6. Fold and glue the spaceship back to back. Punch a hole in the spaceship and the corner of the book. Tie the spaceship to the book. Move the spaceship as you read the book.

Voyage in Space
Have you ever wondered what it is like out in space? Imagine you are an astronaut about to leave Earth. The countdown begins:
1


staple

## Voyage in Space

Have you ever wondered what it is like out in space? Imagine you are an astronaut about to leave Earth. The countdown begins:

**10, 9, 8, 7, 6, 5, 4, 3, 2, 1, blastoff!**

Your ship rises from the launch pad. Up you go, higher and higher. What are you going to see as you travel across the solar system?

Write about your adventure.

1

staple

glue

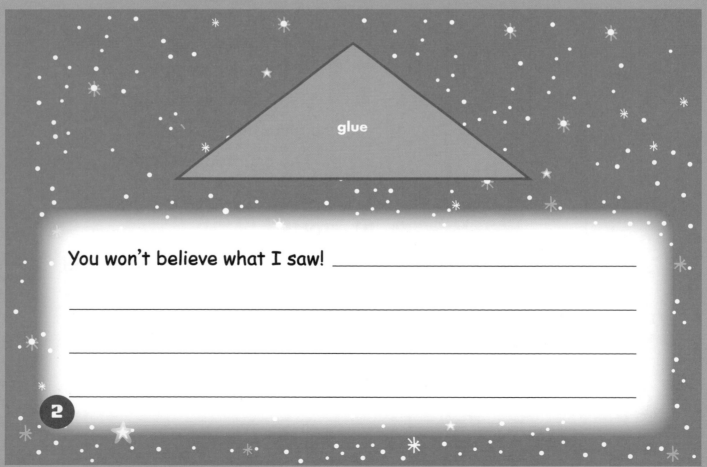

You won't believe what I saw! ______________________________

______________________________

______________________________

______________________________

2

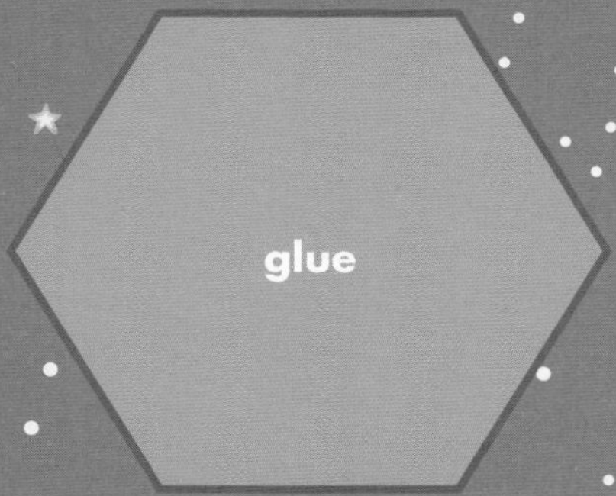
glue

Who is aboard that strange ship? ____________________

______________________________________

______________________________________

______________________________________

3

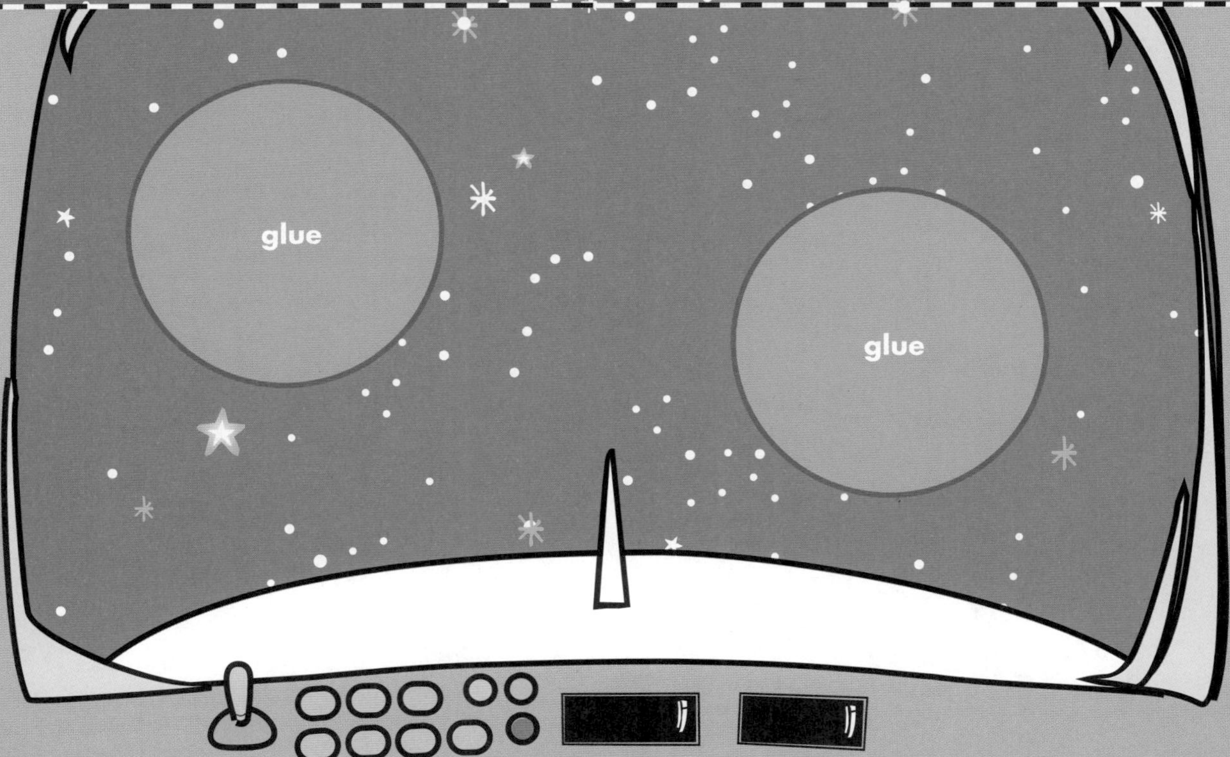
glue
glue

Look out at the dark sky. Earth and the moon shine in the distance. They grow bigger and bigger as my voyage ends.

5

glue

Should I be afraid? ______________________________

__________________________________________________

__________________________________________________

__________________________________________________

4

6

# Eight Planets

Find the planets in the word search.

| | | | | | | | | |
|---|---|---|---|---|---|---|---|---|
| P | V | E | N | U | S | K | Y | U |
| L | I | V | E | A | R | T | H | R |
| U | J | U | P | I | T | E | R | A |
| M | S | A | T | U | R | N | O | N |
| O | U | T | U | M | A | R | S | U |
| P | L | A | N | E | T | S | I | S |
| H | A | M | E | R | C | U | R | Y |

## Word Box

| | | | | |
|---|---|---|---|---|
| Earth | Mars | Neptune | Mercury | Uranus |
| Jupiter | Venus | Saturn | planets | |

SPACE

# Crossword Puzzle

Read the clues.
Write the words in the boxes.

1
2
3
4
5
6
7

## Word Box

astronaut    Earth    Milky Way    moon
planets    stars    sun

## Across

2. the name of our galaxy
5. a traveler in space
7. balls of burning gases

## Down

1. Venus and Mars are ____.
3. We see one ____ in the night sky.
4. the planet we live on
6. the star closest to Earth

# Astronaut

Count by 2s to draw the astronaut.

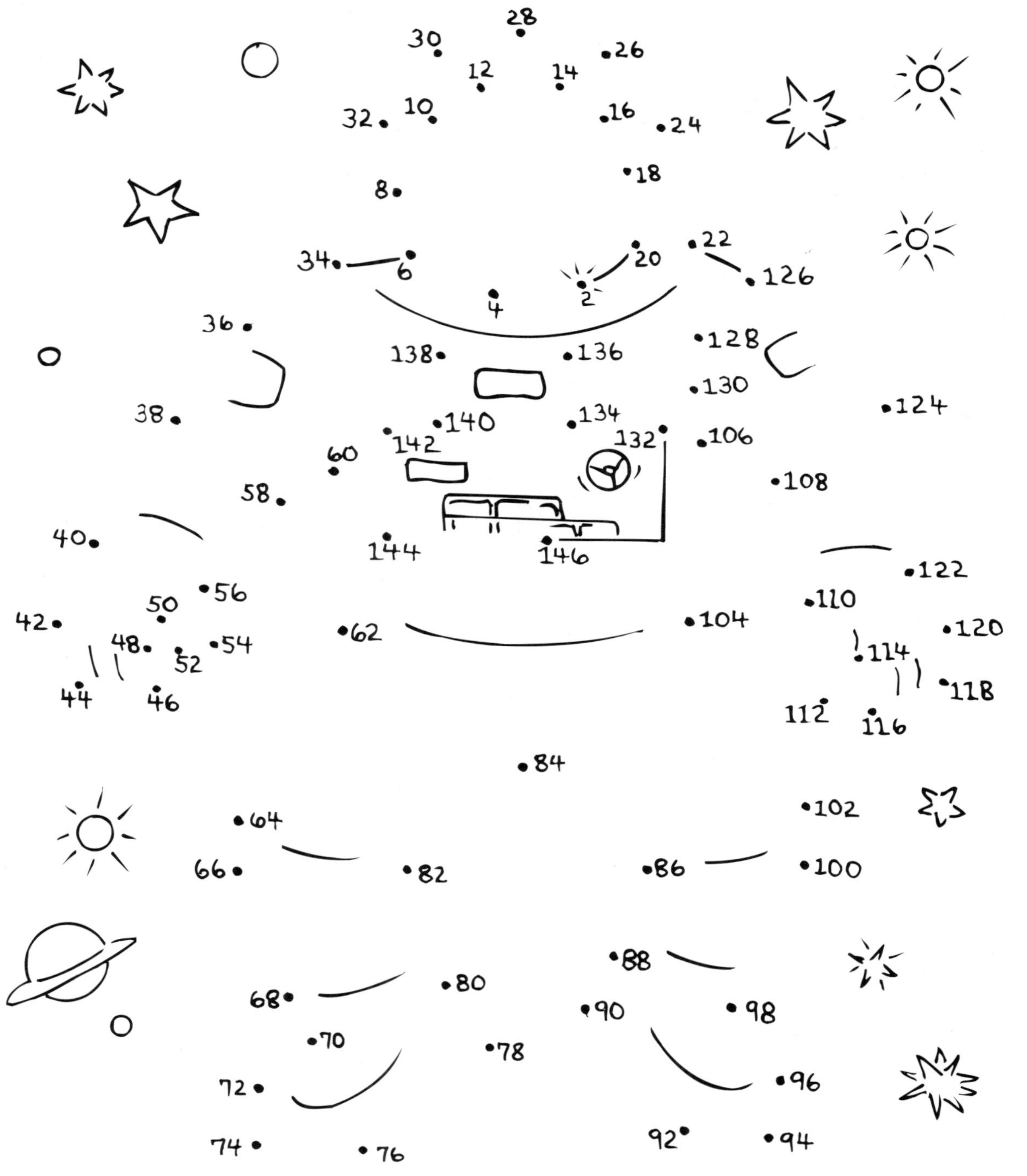

2
4
6
8
10
12
14
16
18
20
22
24
26
28
30
32
34
36
38
40
42
44
46
48
50
52
54
56
58
60
62
64
66
68
70
72
74
76
78
80
82
84
86
88
90
92
94
96
98
100
102
104
106
108
110
112
114
116
118
120
122
124
126
128
130
132
134
136
138
140
142
144
146


Draw your face inside the astronaut's helmet.

# Back to the Ship

Draw a line to help the astronaut get back to the ship.

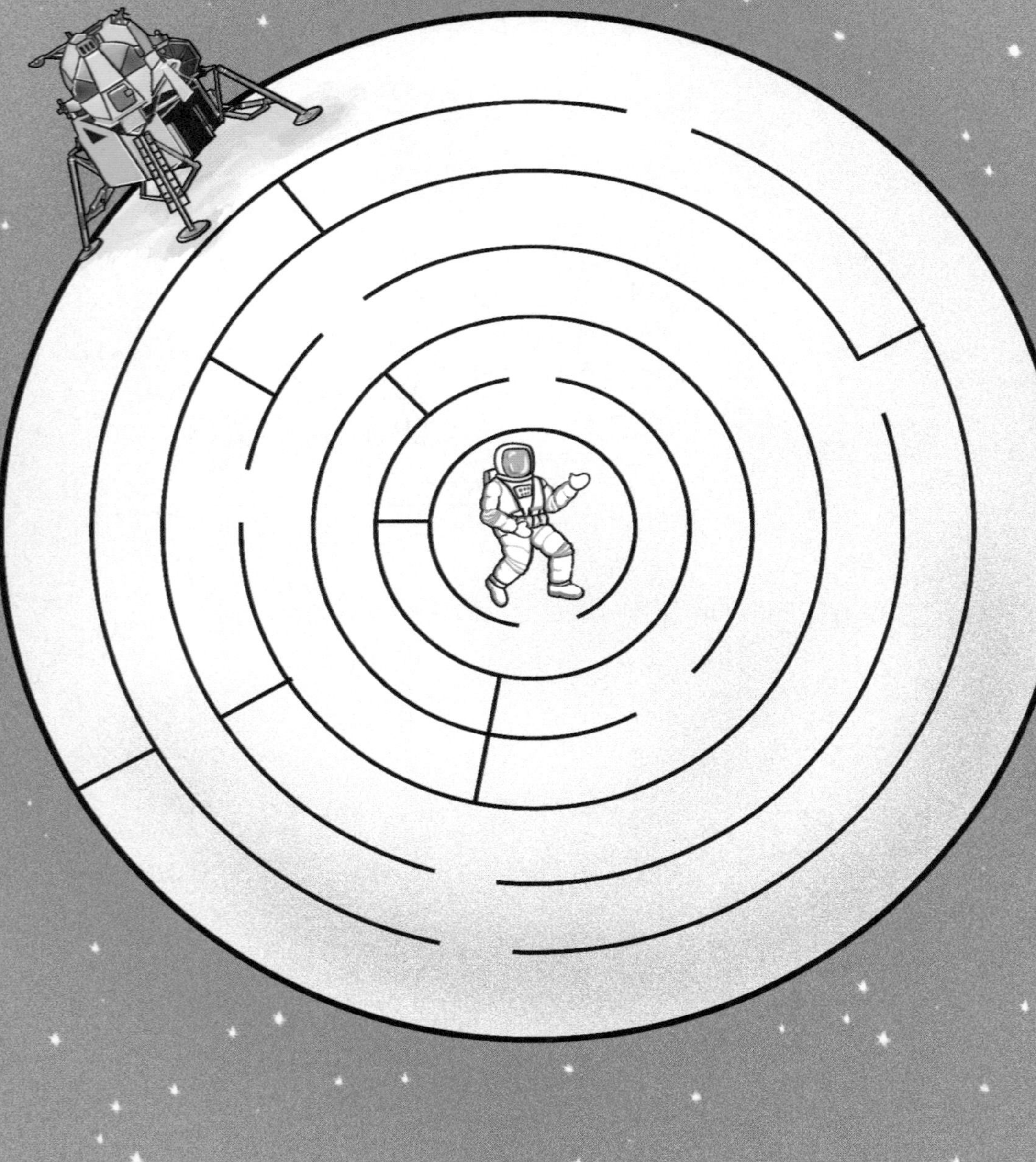

# Start at the Sun

Our **solar system** is the sun and all the bodies that orbit around it: the eight planets, their moons, the asteroids (chunks of rock), and comets (balls of ice and dust). An orbit is the path of a planet or another object around the sun.

Place each planet on its orbit in order from the sun, following these steps:

1. Pull out pages 52, 53, and 55. Glue pages 52 and 53 together.
2. Cut out the planets. Glue them in place on pages 52 and 53.
3. Finish writing the name of each planet in the boxes.

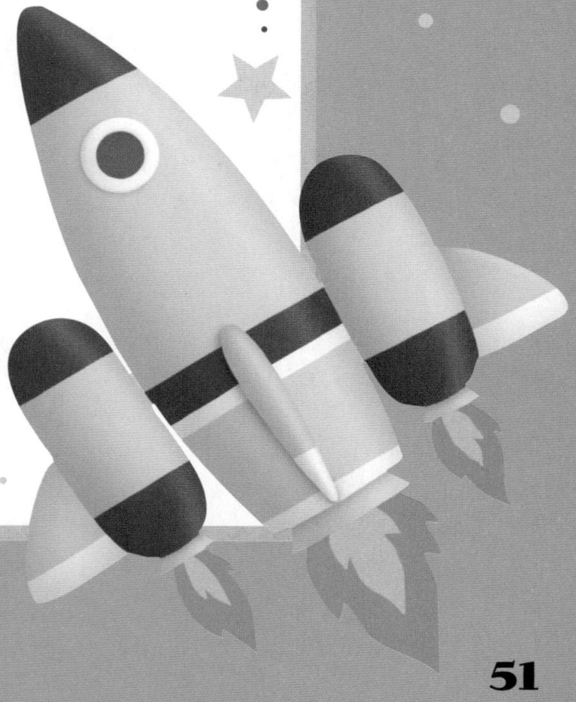

# Our Solar System

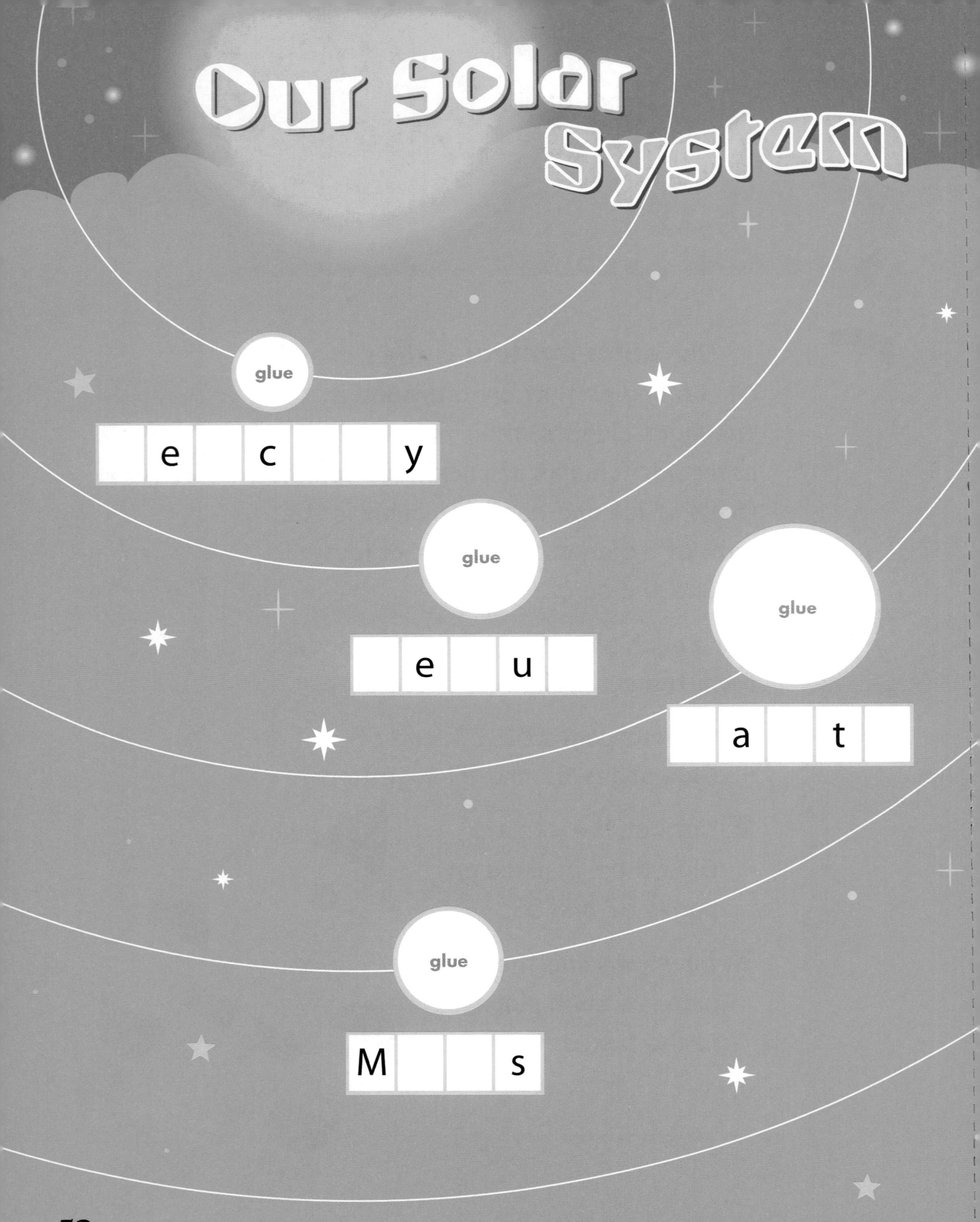

glue
e c y
glue
e u
glue
a t
glue
M s

glue

| | | | | | | |
|---|---|---|---|---|---|---|
| | u | | i | | | r |

glue

| | | | | | |
|---|---|---|---|---|---|
| | r | | n | | s |

glue

| | | | | | | |
|---|---|---|---|---|---|---|
| | e | p | t | | | e |

glue

| | | | | | |
|---|---|---|---|---|---|
| | a | | u | | |

# Planets

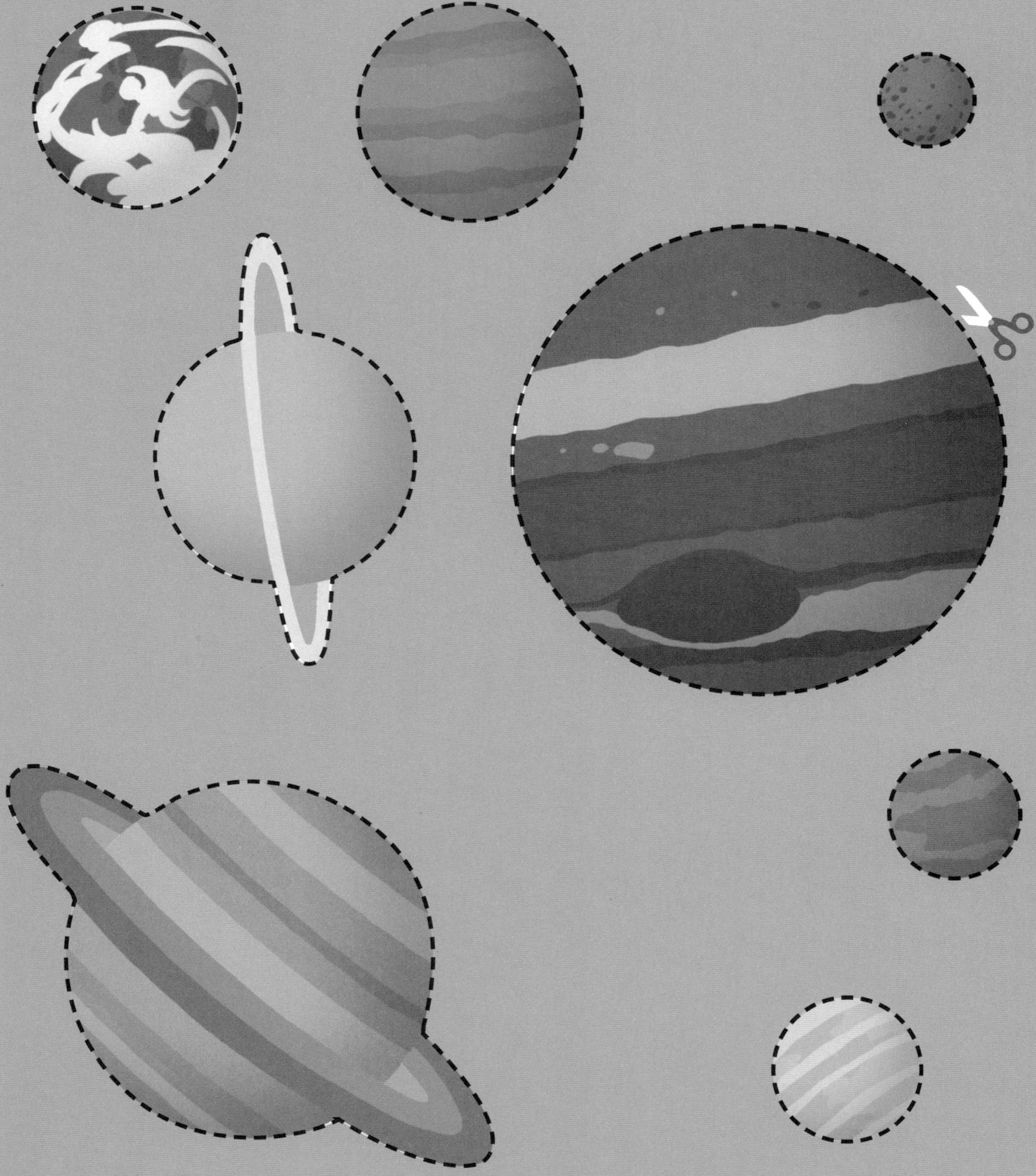

# Spaceship

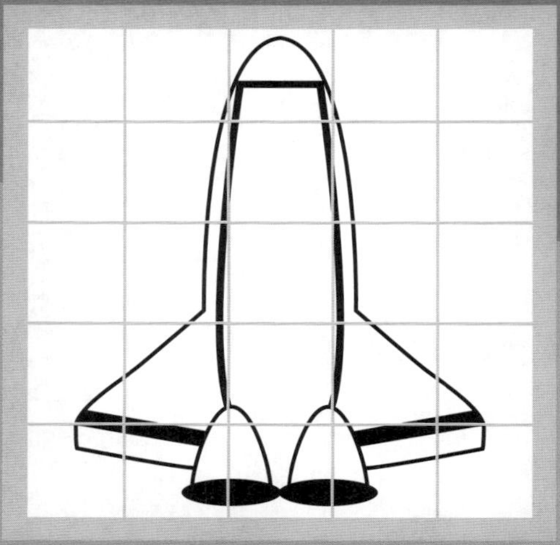

Draw and color this spaceship.

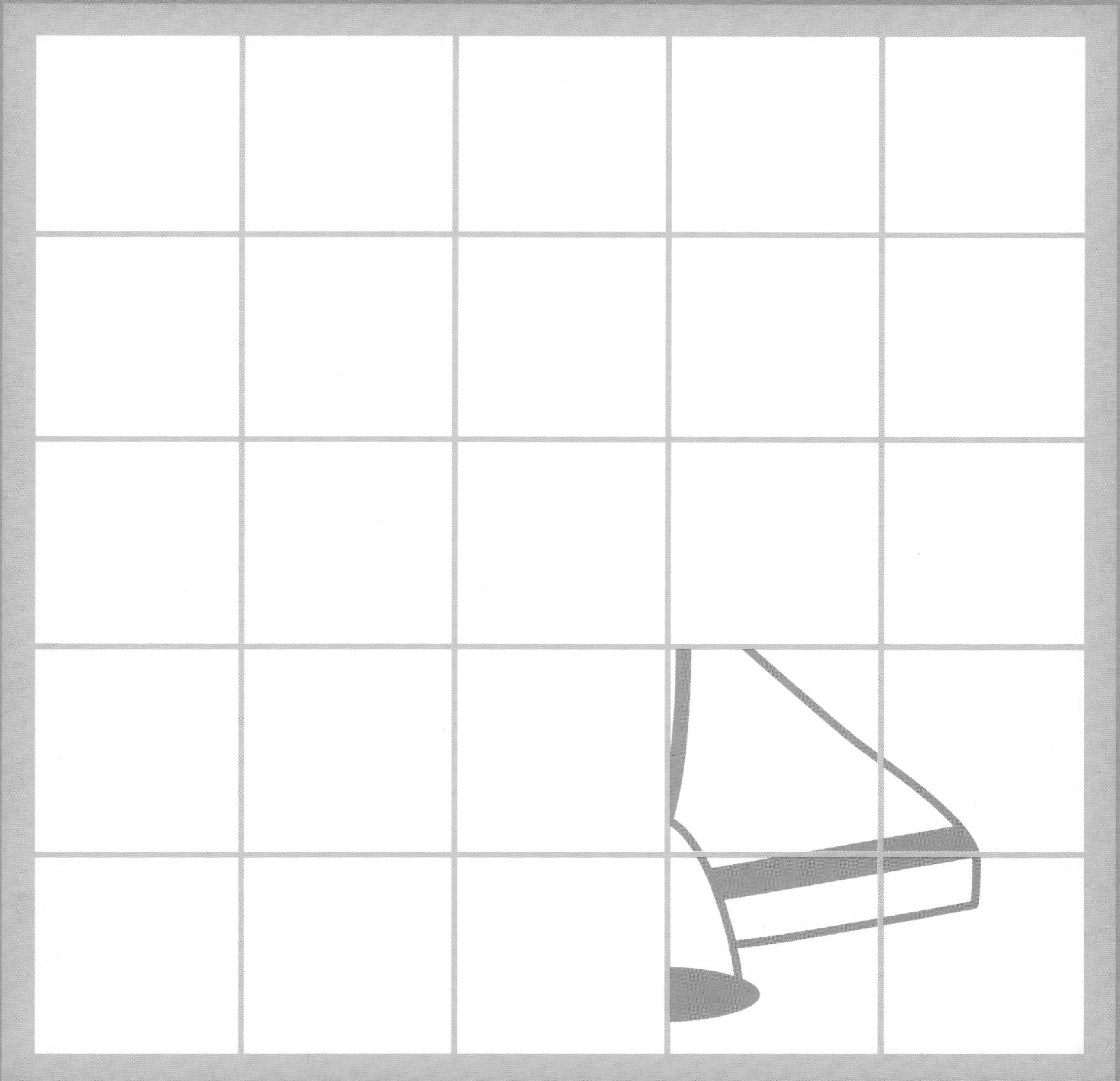

# Name the Astronaut

Use the code to help you answer the riddles.

| | | | | |
|---|---|---|---|---|
| 1—A | 4—G | 7—M | 10—R | 13—Y |
| 2—D | 5—I | 8—N | 11—S | |
| 3—E | 6—L | 9—O | 12—T | |

Who was the first American woman in space?

__ __ __ __ __   __ __ __ __
11 1 6 6 13   10 5 2 3

Who was the first man to set foot on the moon?

__ __ __ __
8 3 5 6

__ __ __ __ __ __ __ __ __
1 10 7 11 12 10 9 8 4

# Voyager

Voyager is a space probe. It is one way scientists have explored the planets. Count by 2s to connect the dots to see Voyager.

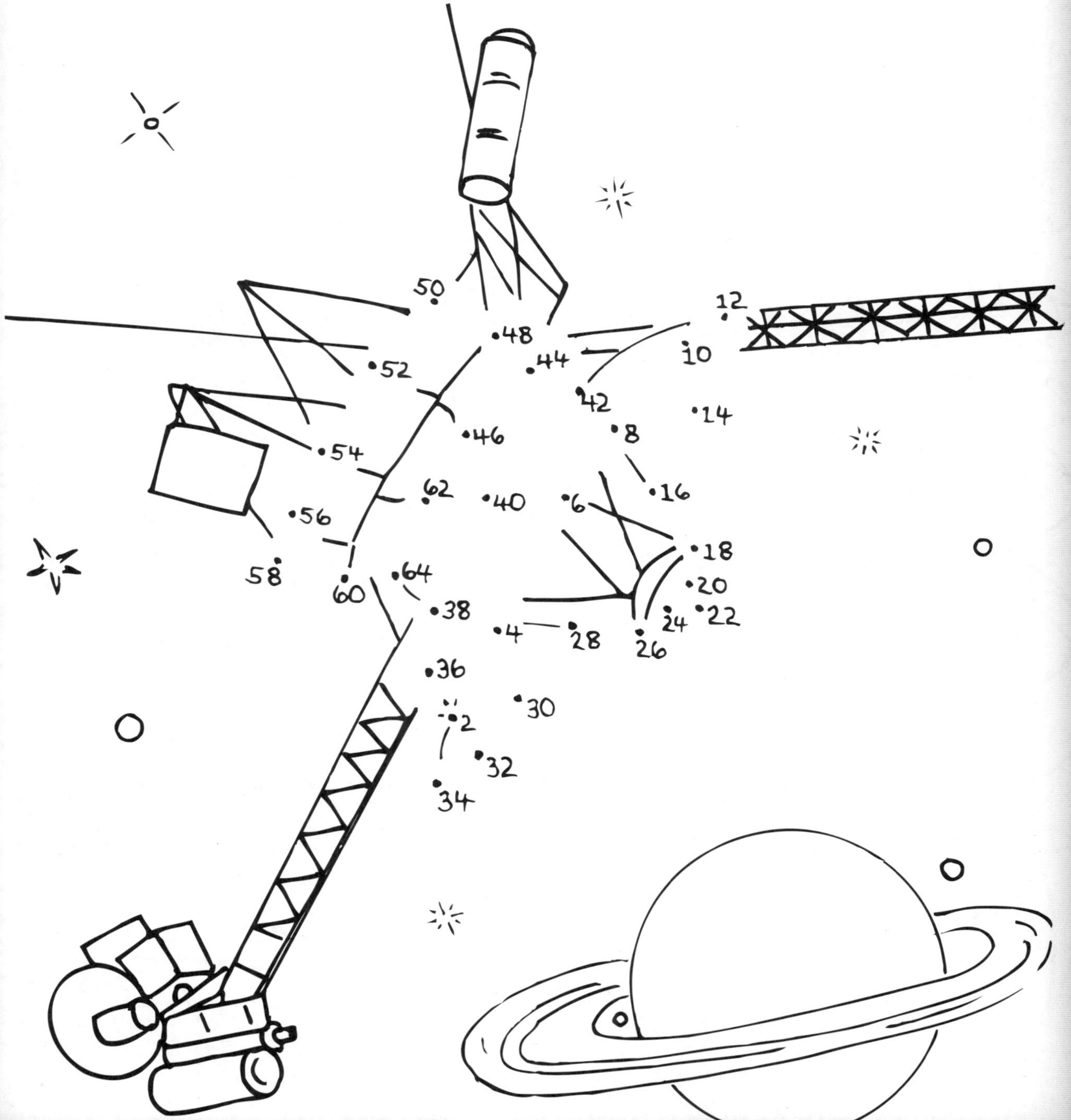

50
12
48
10
44
52
42
14
46
8
54
62
40
6
16
56
18
58
60
64
20
38
24
22
4
28
26
36
30
2
32
34

# Space Aliens

Find the space aliens hiding on the moon. Color them.

How many aliens did you find?

# In the Rainforest

Find these rainforest animals in the word search.

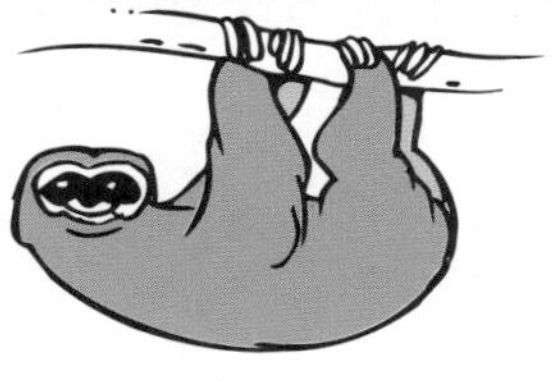

Sloth

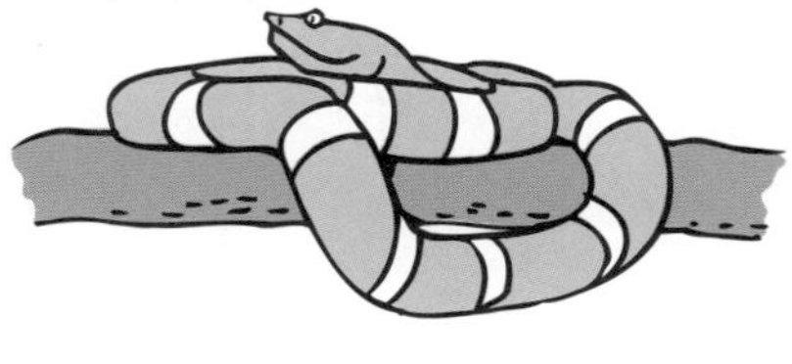

Boa Constrictor

Jaguar

Toucan

Anteater

Tapir

Bat

Poison Dart Frog

Howler Monkey

| | | | | | | | | | | | | | |
|---|---|---|---|---|---|---|---|---|---|---|---|---|---|
| H | O | W | L | E | R | M | O | N | K | E | Y | T | O |
| B | O | A | C | O | N | S | T | R | I | C | T | O | R |
| A | B | R | A | I | N | Y | T | M | S | X | O | W | C |
| N | J | A | G | U | A | R | A | Z | L | P | U | N | H |
| A | Q | R | T | Y | Z | F | P | D | O | W | C | B | I |
| N | A | M | A | Z | O | N | I | O | T | E | A | E | D |
| A | N | T | E | A | T | E | R | G | H | T | N | O | W |
| P | O | I | S | O | N | D | A | R | T | F | R | O | G |

**Can you find these rainforest plants?** banana fig orchid

# Sloth

I am one of the slowest animals in the rainforest. Count by 10s to connect the dots.

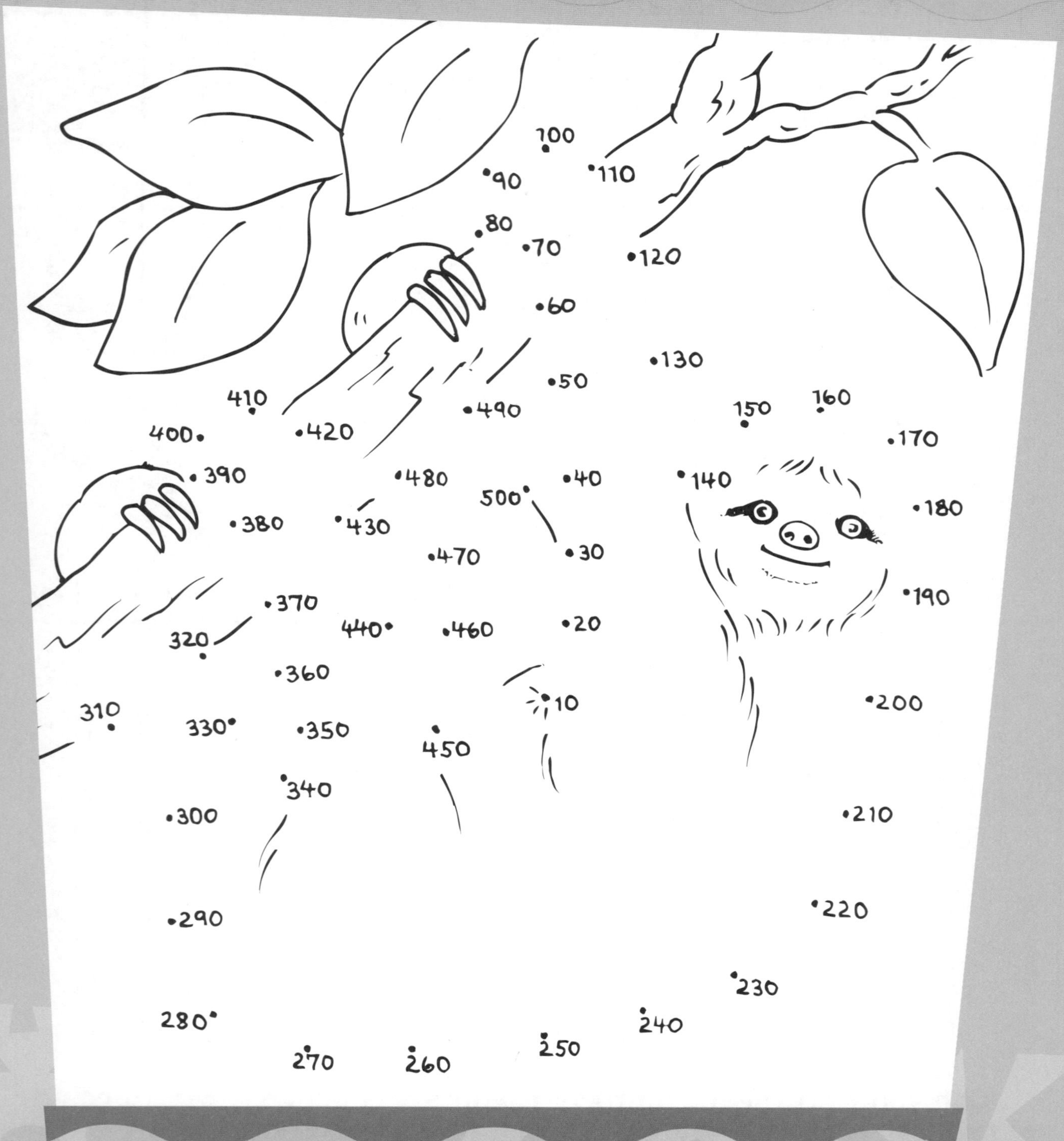

10
20
30
40
50
60
70
80
90
100
110
120
130
140
150
160
170
180
190
200
210
220
230
240
250
260
270
280
290
300
310
320
330
340
350
360
370
380
390
400
410
420
430
440
450
460
470
480
490
500

# Rainforest Animals

Color the rainforest animals.

# Who Am I?

Use the code to answer the riddles.
Then draw a line from the riddle to the correct animal.

A E H M P T
C F I N R U
D G L O S X

1. I am a colorful rainforest bird. Who am I?

2. I am slow-moving. I hang upside down from tree branches. Who am I?

3. I use my sticky tongue to catch and eat insects. Who am I?

4. My bright color warns other animals to leave me alone. Who am I?

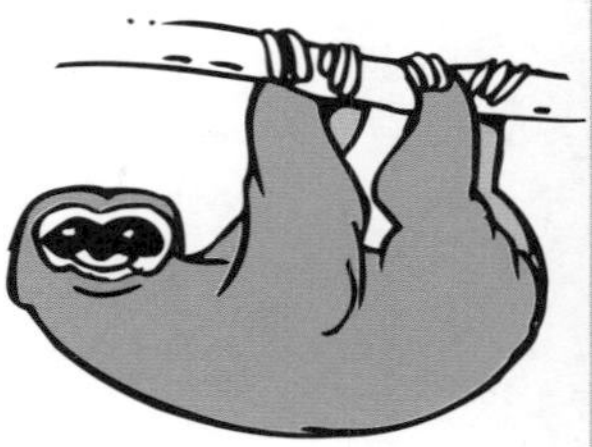

# Leaf-Cutter Ant

Draw a line to guide the leaf-cutter ant back to its nest.

START
END

# Toucan

Follow these steps to draw and color a toucan.
Draw it on page 67.

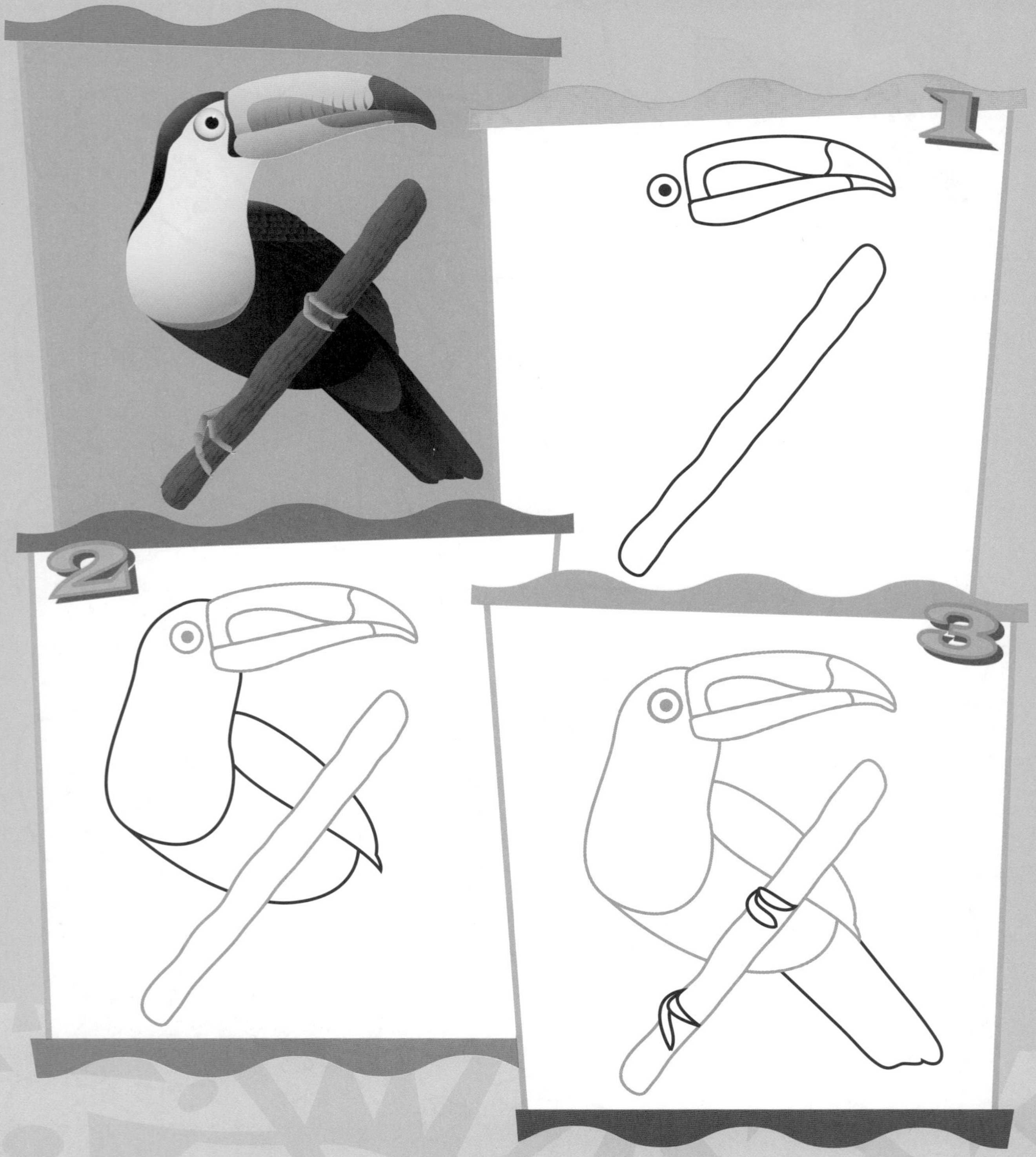
1
2
3

A toucan lives in the rainforest. It is a very large bird. It has a huge beak. Fruit is a toucan's favorite food. It also eats bird eggs, insects, and tree frogs.

# Colorful Frogs and Snakes

Color each animal differently.

Poison dart frogs come in many bright colors. The colors are a warning that says "Don't eat me!"

There are snakes of many colors and designs in the rainforest.

# Emerald Tree Boa

Cut out the snake on the dotted line. Wrap it around your arm or leg.

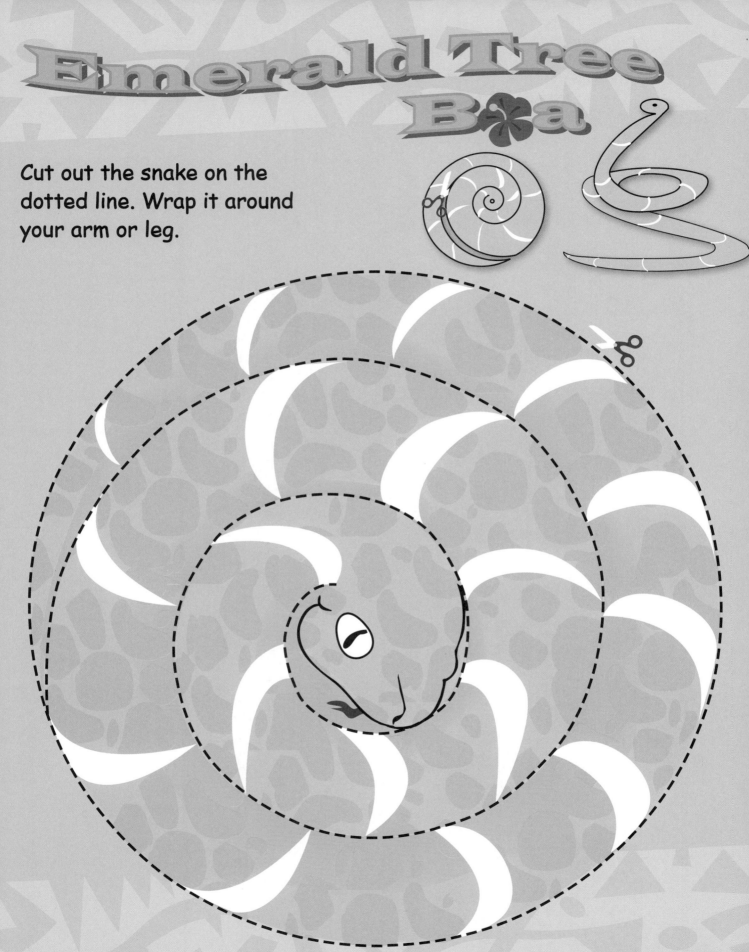

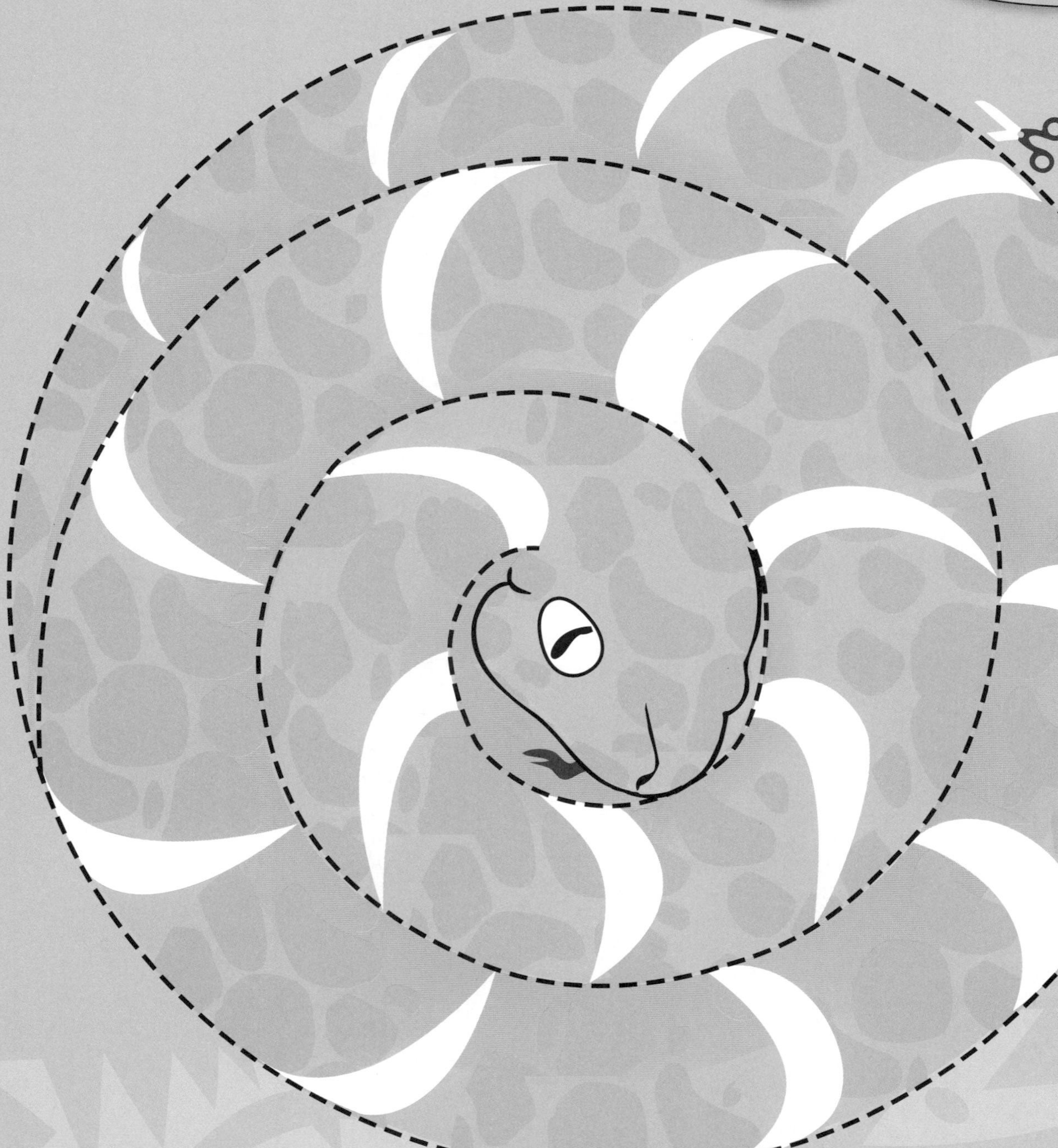

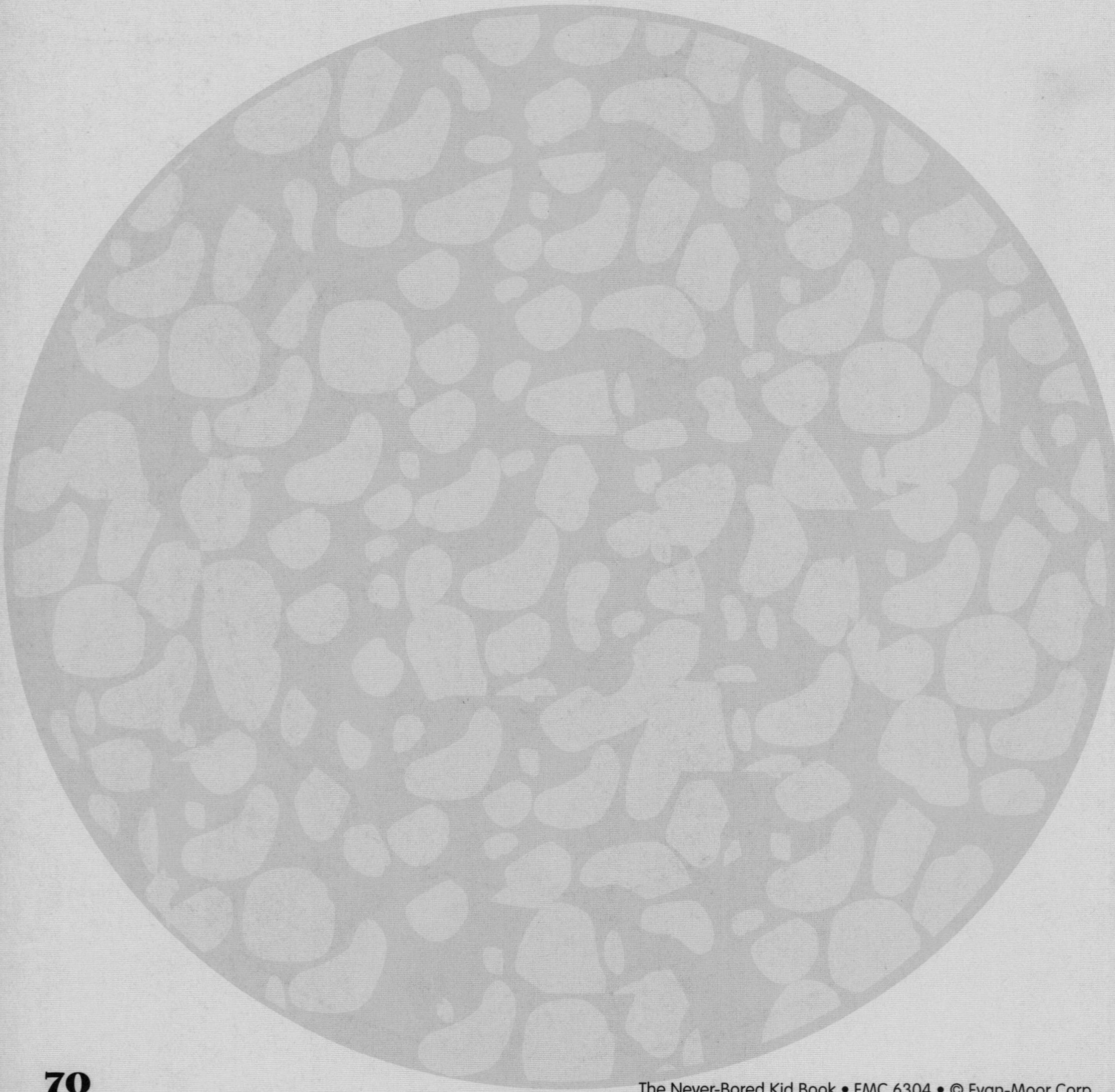

# Treasure Map

Cut out the puzzle pieces. Put the puzzle together.
Glue the pieces inside the frame on page 73.

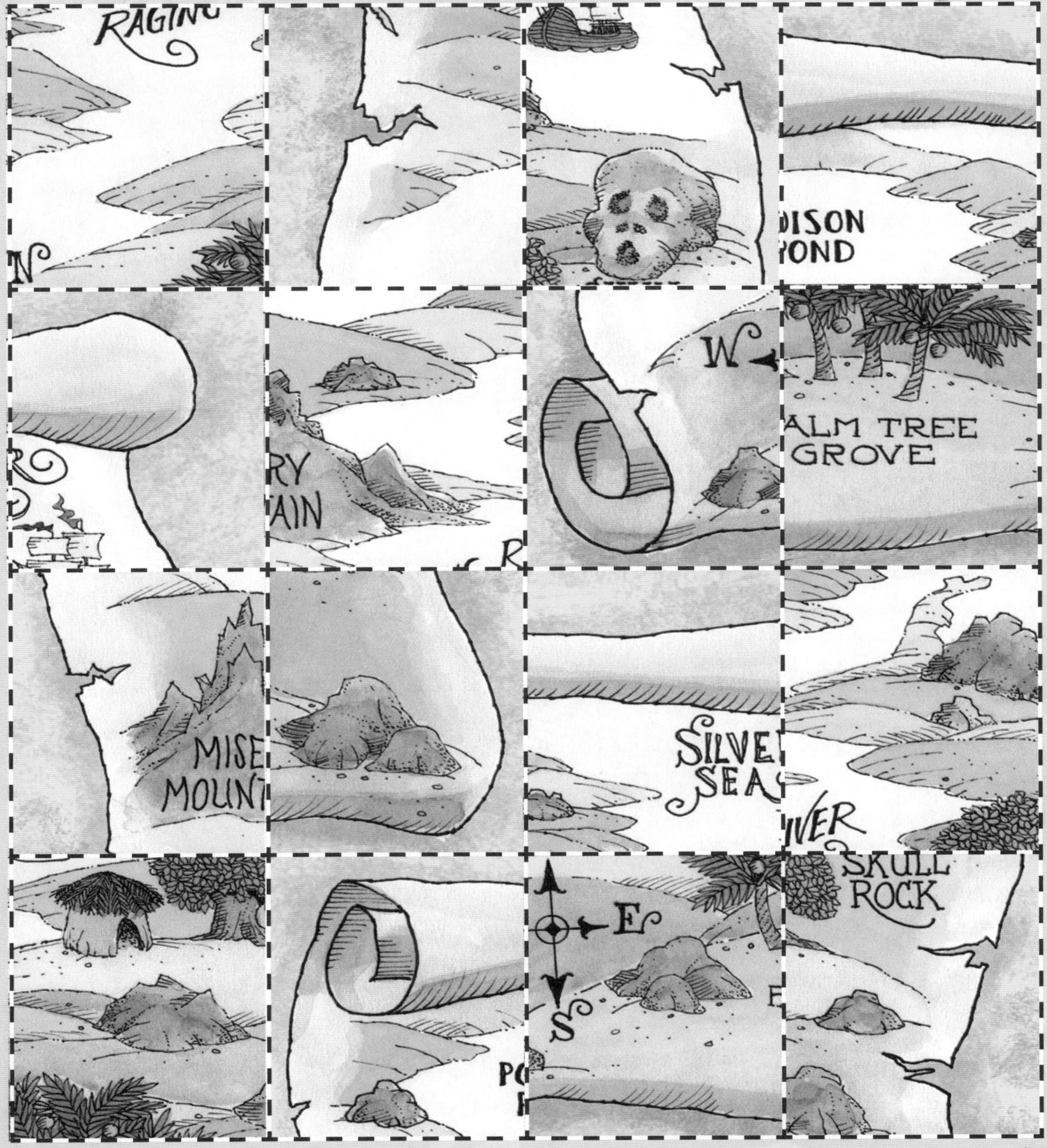
RAGING
DISON
POND
W
ALM TREE
GROVE
RY
AIN
MISE
MOUNT
SILVE
SEA
IVER
SKULL
ROCK
E
S

# Treasure Map

| | | | |
|---|---|---|---|
| glue | glue | glue | glue |
| glue | glue | glue | glue |
| glue | glue | glue | glue |
| glue | glue | glue | glue |

# All Aboard!

Start at 1. Connect the dots. Color the picture.

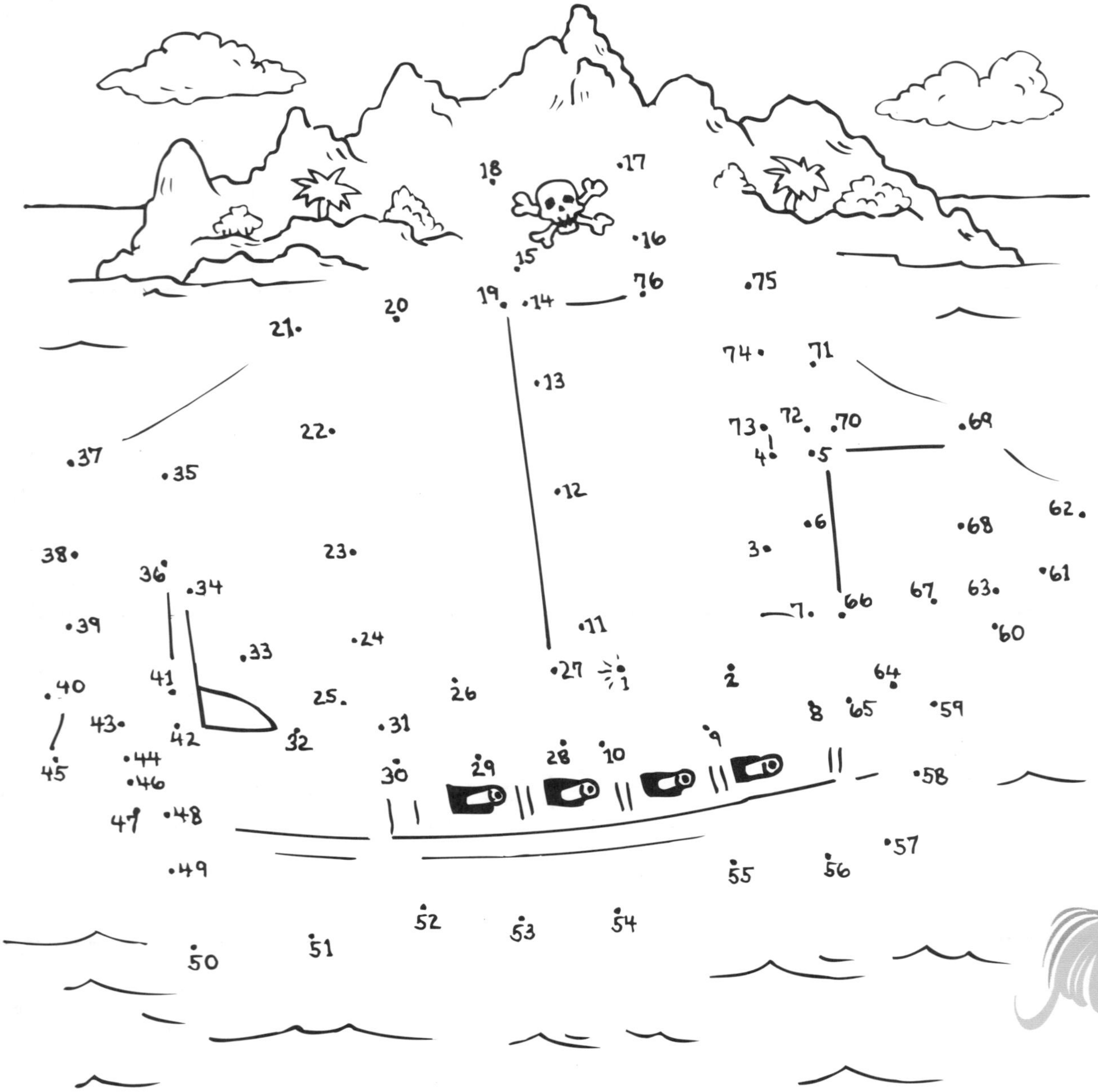

Blackbeard and his pirate crew are sailing off after treasure.

What do you think they will find? ______________________________

______________________________________________________________

# Treasure Hunt

Help Blackbeard the Pirate find the treasure chest.

# Peg-Leg Pete

Follow these steps to draw and color a pirate.
Draw the pirate on the deck of his ship on page 77.

How do you think Peg-Leg Pete lost his leg?

# Pirates

Find the hidden words.

| | | | | | | | | | | | | |
|---|---|---|---|---|---|---|---|---|---|---|---|---|
| P | I | R | A | T | E | D | A | G | G | E | R | X |
| C | R | O | S | S | B | O | N | E | S | P | S | A |
| A | P | S | K | U | L | C | D | O | U | A | I | N |
| P | Q | L | H | Z | Z | A | R | T | J | C | L | C |
| T | Z | T | E | I | U | N | X | E | E | T | V | H |
| A | M | M | N | T | P | N | R | X | W | A | E | O |
| I | M | A | R | S | W | O | R | D | E | I | R | R |
| N | D | I | P | W | Z | N | Z | N | L | N | X | Q |
| T | R | E | A | S | U | R | E | C | H | E | S | T |
| G | O | L | D | D | O | U | B | L | O | O | N | S |

## Word Box

- anchor
- captain
- cannon
- crew
- crossbones
- dagger
- doubloons
- gold
- jewel
- map
- pirate
- ship
- silver
- sword
- treasure chest

# Skull and Crossbones

When you see this flying over a ship, look out!
Start at 1. Connect the dots. Color the picture.

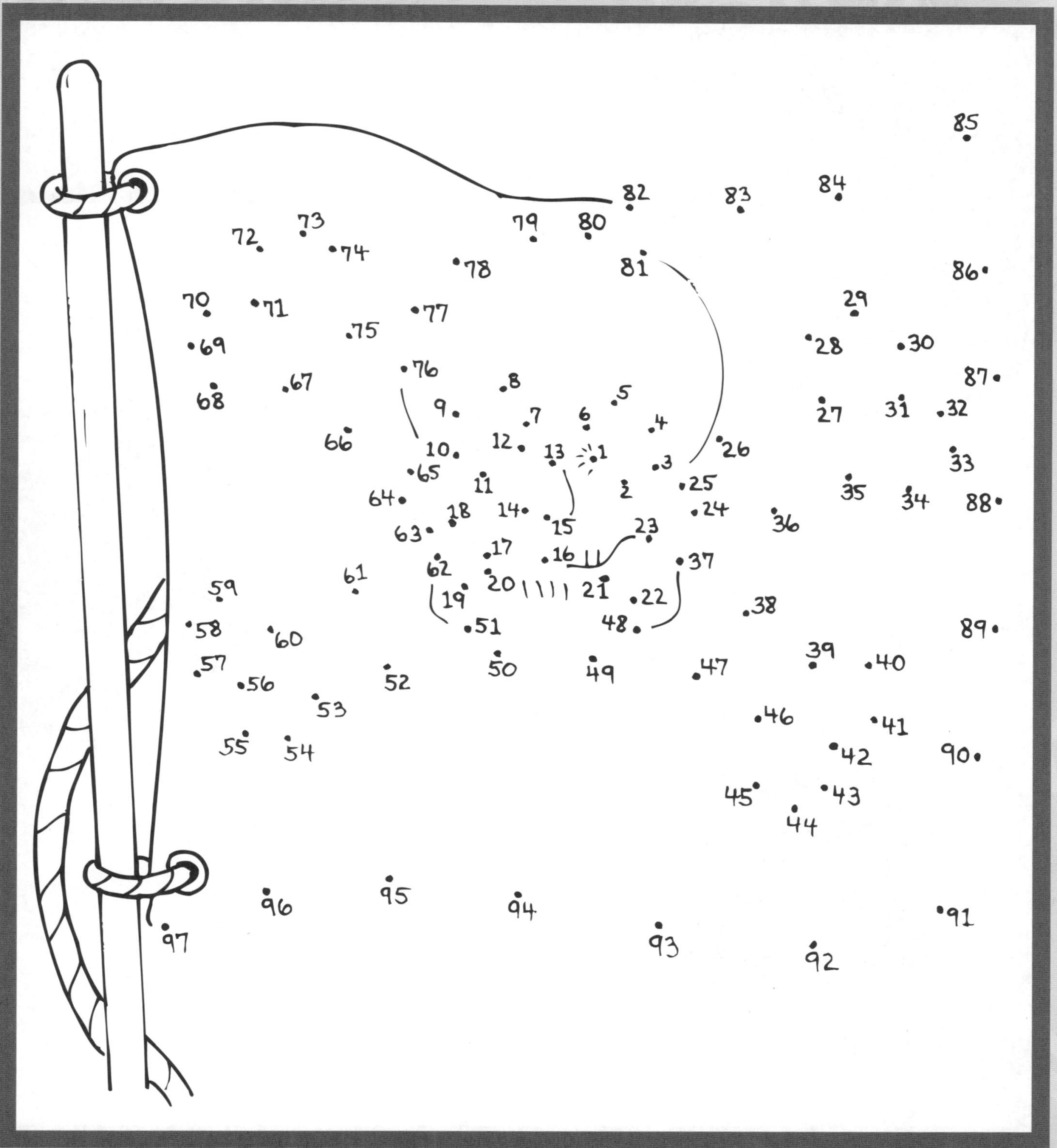

# Name the Pirates

Use the code to name the pirates.

| | a | b | c | d | e |
|---|---|---|---|---|---|
| 1 | A | B | C | D | E |
| 2 | H | I | K | L | N |
| 3 | O | P | R | T | |

1c 1a 3b 3d 1a 2b 2e

2a 3a 3a 2c

1b 2d 1a 1c 2c 1b 1e 1a 3c 1d

1c 1a 3b 3d 1a 2b 2e

2c 2b 1d 1d

# In the Treasure Chest

1. Remove pages 81 and 83 from the book.
2. Cut out the treasure chest on page 83. Fold it on the lines. Staple it on the sides.
3. Cut out the treasure below. Put it in the chest.

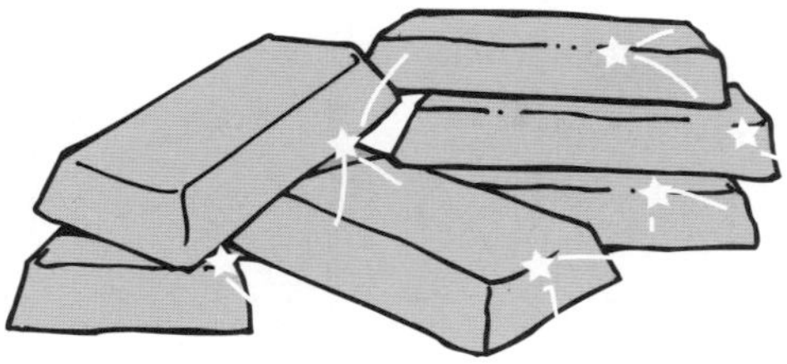

Bars of gold weigh a ton.
They will pay for so much fun.

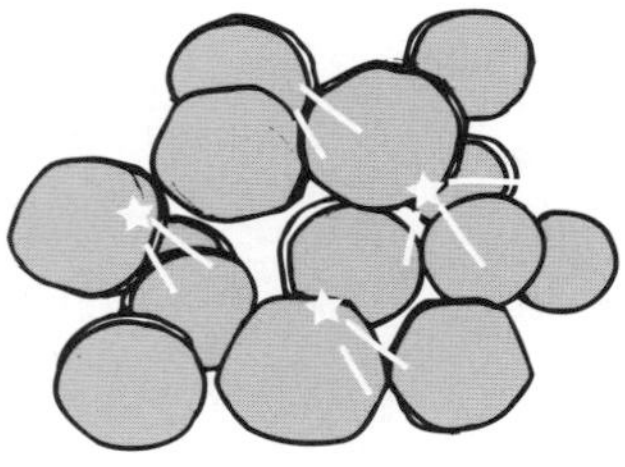

Doubloons! What are they?
Coins for a pirate's pay.

With a silver dagger in my hand,
I could fight a pirate band.

A pile of jewels of every kind!
There are so many. What a find!

A circle of gold with precious stones—It's a crown any king would want to own.

The prettiest pearl necklace ever seen—It would be perfect for a queen.

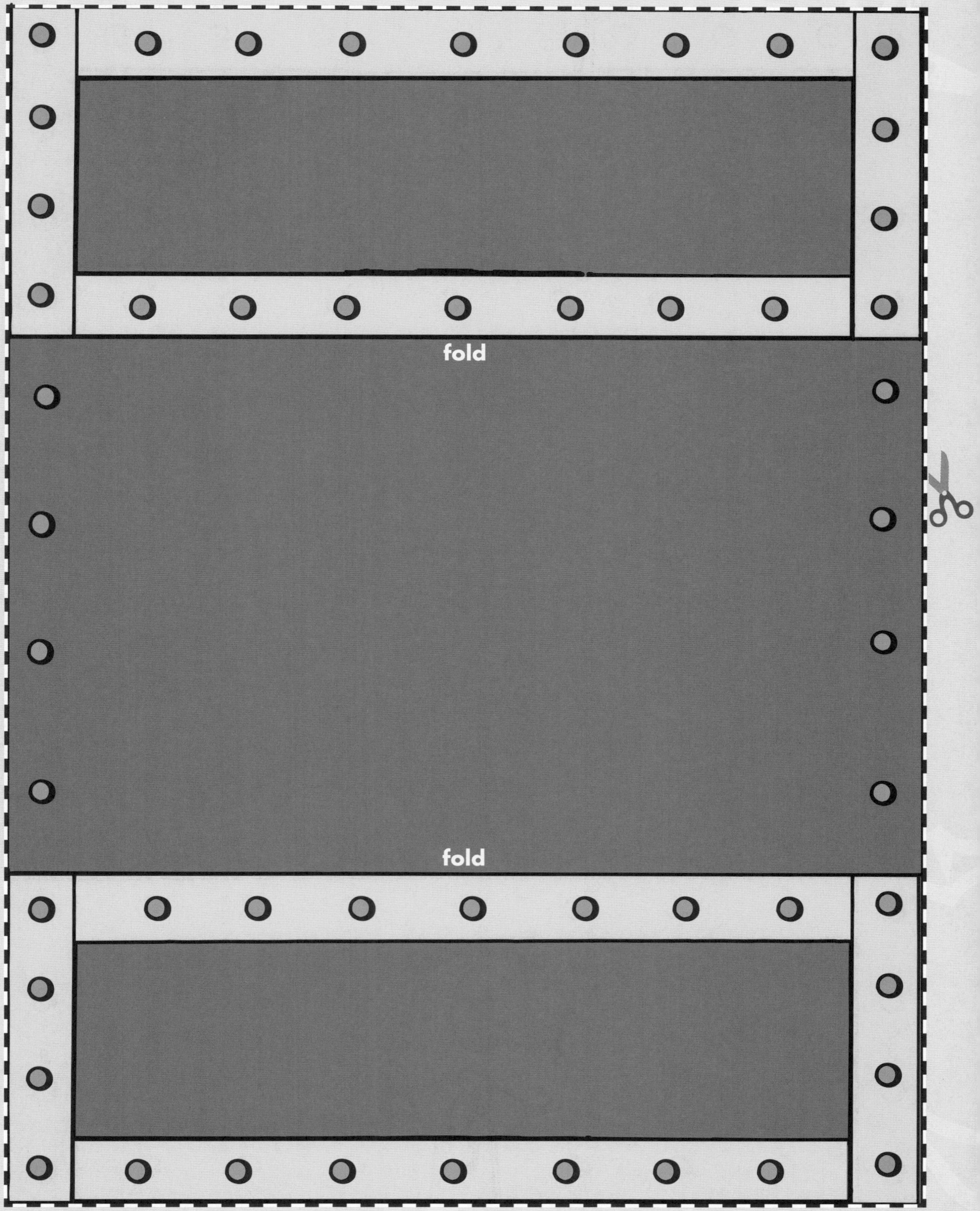
fold
fold

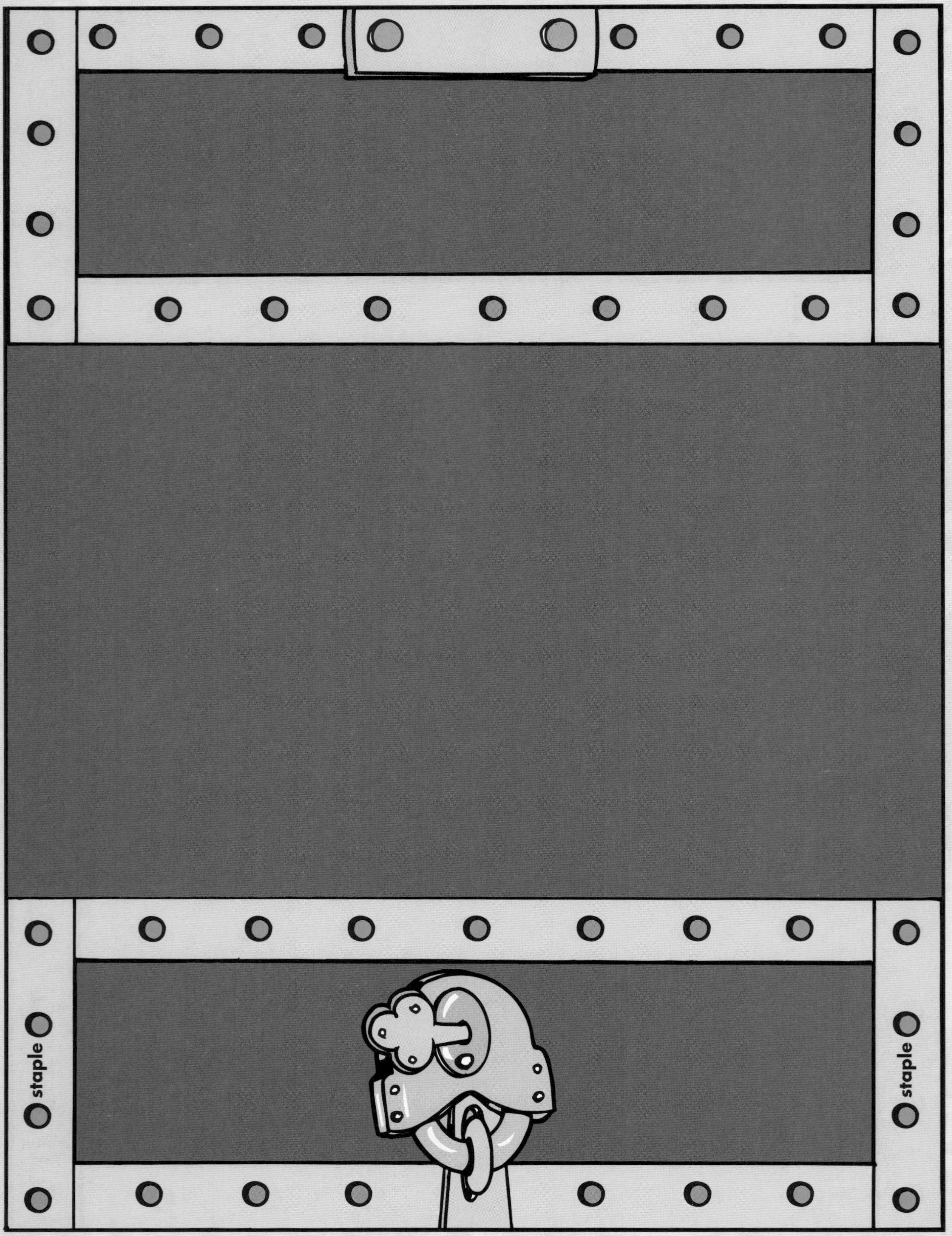
staple
staple

# Pop, Pop, Popcorn

Get out the oil.
Pour some in the pot.
Plop go the kernels.
Now, wait until it's hot.

Pop goes the first kernel.
Pop goes the next.
Then pop, pop...explosion
There go all the rest!

Linda Holliman

# Making Popcorn

Cut out page 87. Glue the steps in order.

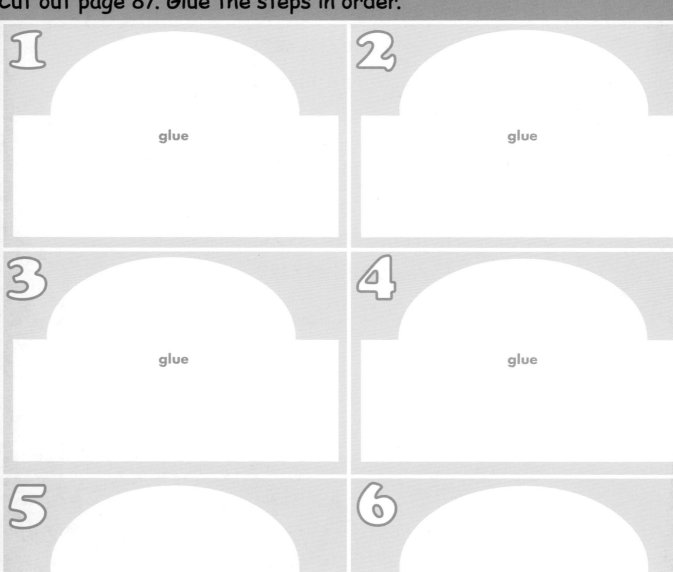

| | |
|---|---|
| 1<br>glue | 2<br>glue |
| 3<br>glue | 4<br>glue |
| 5<br>glue | 6<br>glue |

Wait for the kernels to pop.

Start the popper.

Pour kernels into the popcorn popper.

Get the popcorn from the cupboard.

Eat the popcorn.

Salt

Pour melted butter and salt on the popped corn.

# Popcorn Pair

Find the matching kernels.

# Where's the Popcorn?

Draw a line from the girl to the clown selling popcorn.

# A Fable

Cut out the storybook. Staple the pages together in order.

staple

# The Grasshopper and the Ants

It was summertime, and the days were warm and bright. The fields were filled with insects. A grasshopper was hopping about the field. He saw a line of ants passing by. The ants were carrying seeds. The grasshopper said, "Come play with me. Let's have some fun!"

staple

1

But the busy ants kept moving as they called out to him, "We can't stop now. Work must be done!"

Every day, the grasshopper spent his time hopping along and singing. And every day he saw the ants carrying seeds to their nest.

2

One day, the grasshopper asked an ant, "Why are you working so hard? You could be playing in the warm sun."

"I am helping to store food for the winter," said the ant. "I think you should do the same."

"Why bother," said the grasshopper as he hopped away to play. "There is plenty of food to eat."

3

When winter came, the ants were never hungry. They ate the food they had stored during the summer. But the poor grasshopper could find nothing to eat. "Now I see why the ants worked so hard," cried the grasshopper. "When you have a lot, you should save some for later."

4

# Ant and a Grasshopper

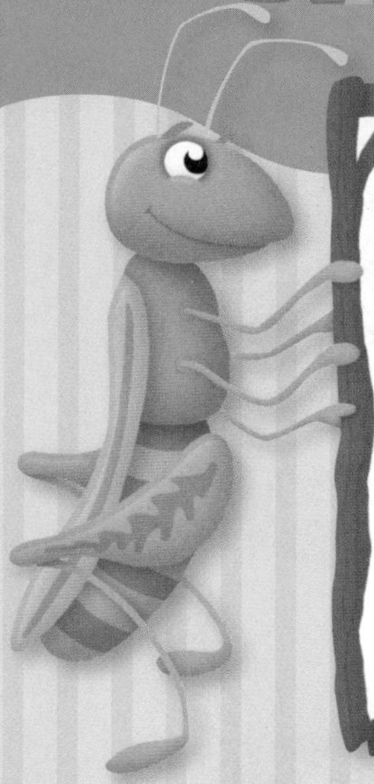

Both an ant and a grasshopper are insects. Insects are alike in these ways:

- six legs
- two antennae
- three body parts
  - head
  - chest (thorax)
  - stomach (abdomen)

Label the parts of this ant.

How many legs does an ant have?

# Insect Concentration

## (a game for 2)

### Make the game.

1. Remove pages 97, 99, and 101 from the book.
2. Cut the cards apart.

### Play the game.

1. Mix up the cards.
2. Lay the cards picture side down.
3. Take turns turning over two cards at a time. If the cards are the same, you keep them. If the cards are not the same, turn them back over.
4. When all the cards have been matched, count your cards. The person with the most cards is the winner.

Butterfly
Dragonfly
Grasshopper
Ladybug

Butterfly

Butterfly

Bumblebee

Bumblebee

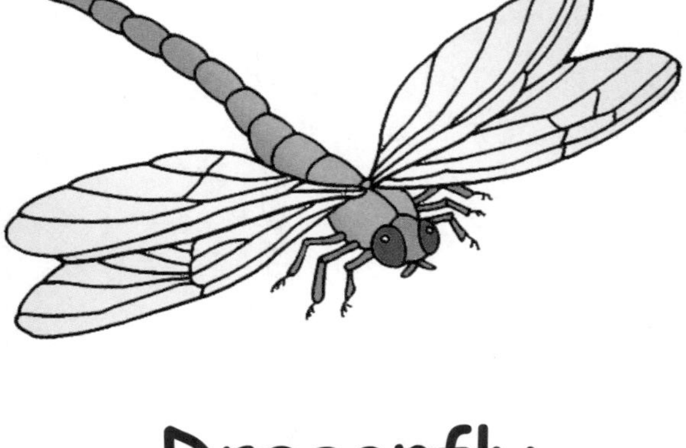

Dragonfly

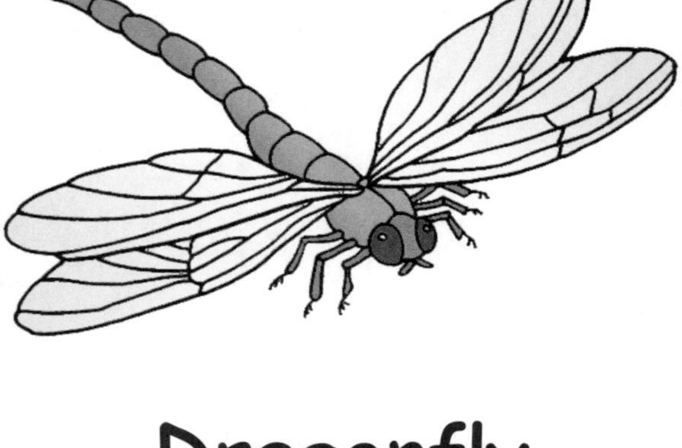

Dragonfly

Ladybug

Ladybug

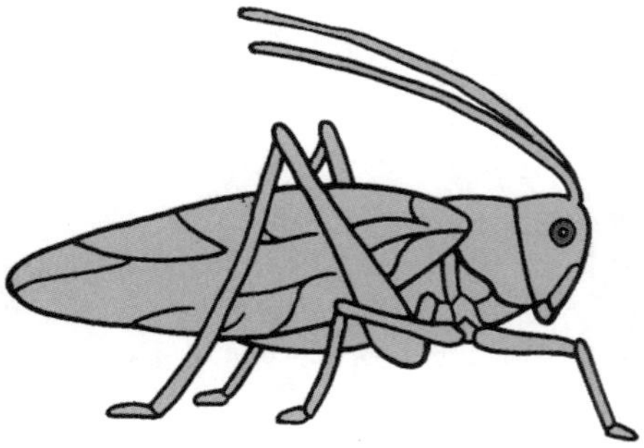

Grasshopper

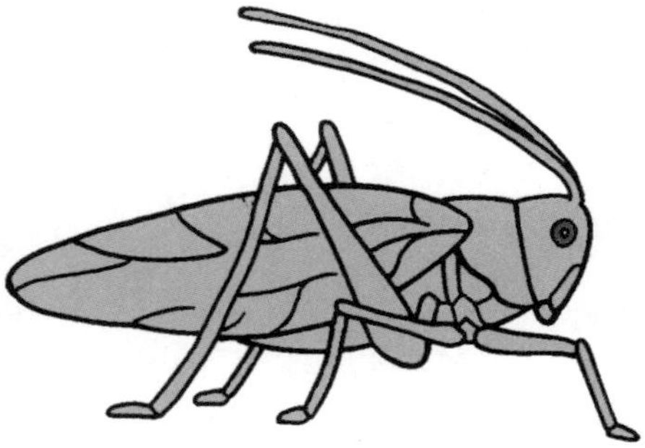

Grasshopper

Water Bug

Water Bug

Moth

Moth

Praying Mantis

Praying Mantis

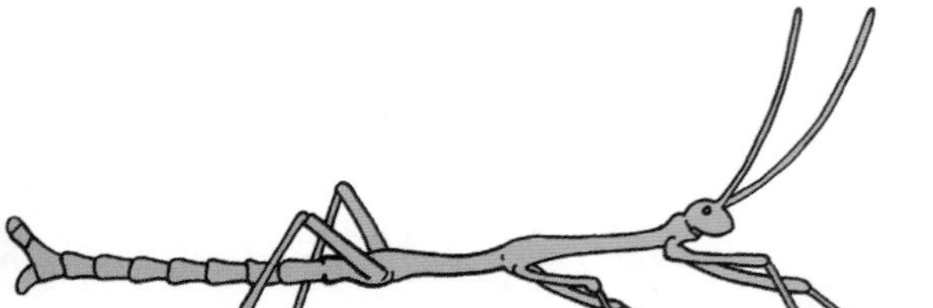

Walking Stick

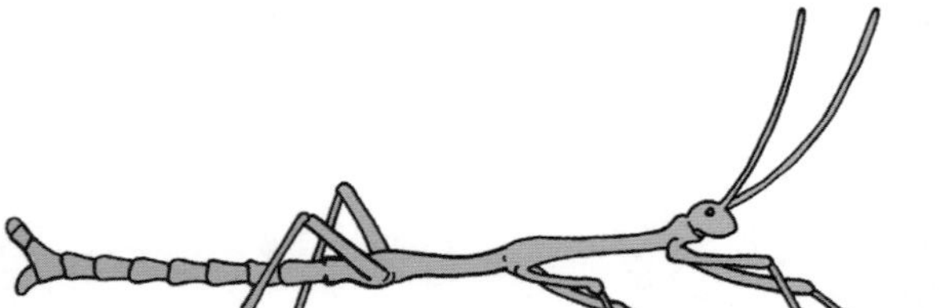

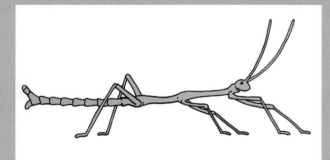

Walking Stick

# Insects

Find the insects in the word search. Circle them.

| | | | | | | | | | | | |
|---|---|---|---|---|---|---|---|---|---|---|---|
| G | R | A | S | S | H | O | P | P | E | R | B |
| B | A | X | M | A | Y | F | O | X | G | D | E |
| U | P | N | B | O | U | T | L | M | C | R | E |
| M | E | E | T | E | T | H | E | Y | R | A | T |
| B | F | W | I | C | D | H | O | T | I | G | L |
| L | L | L | A | D | Y | B | U | G | C | O | E |
| E | E | G | O | S | X | Z | U | Z | K | N | G |
| B | A | C | A | T | P | P | I | G | E | F | N |
| E | S | T | I | N | K | B | U | G | T | L | A |
| E | B | U | T | T | E | R | F | L | Y | Y | T |

## Word Box

| | | |
|---|---|---|
| ant | cricket | grasshopper |
| bedbug | dragonfly | ladybug |
| beetle | flea | moth |
| bumblebee | fly | stink bug |
| butterfly | gnat | wasp |

# Who Am I?

A
E
K
N
S
Y
B
G
L
P
T
D
I
M
R
U


Use the code to name the insects.
Then draw a line from each name to the insect.

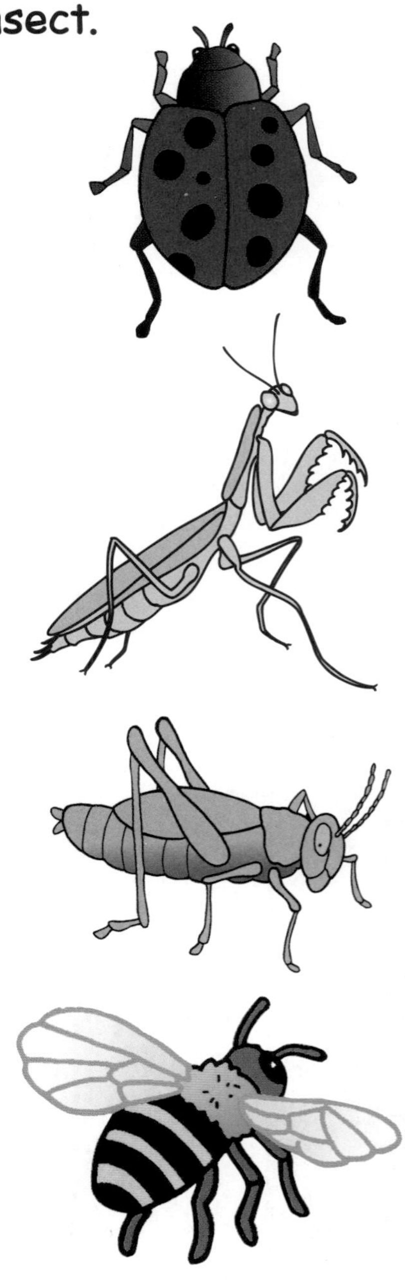

1.

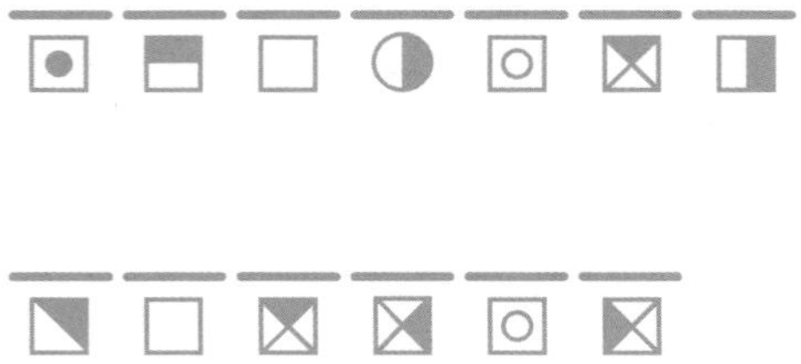

2.

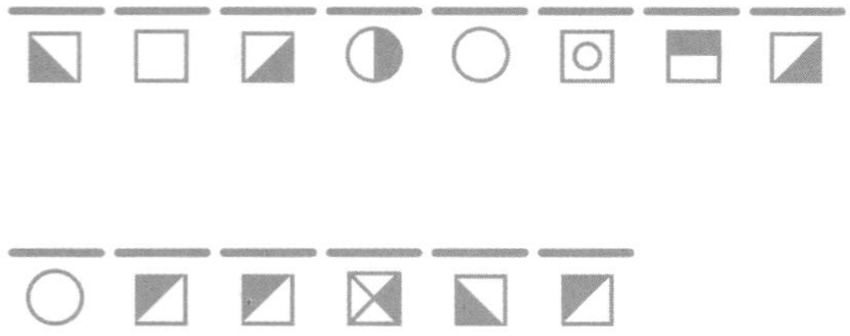

3.

4.

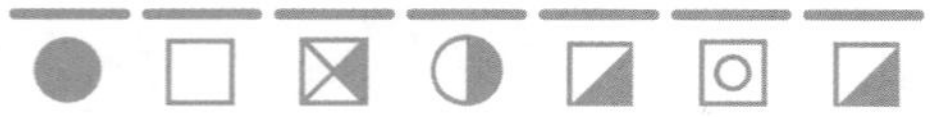

# A Really Big Butterfly

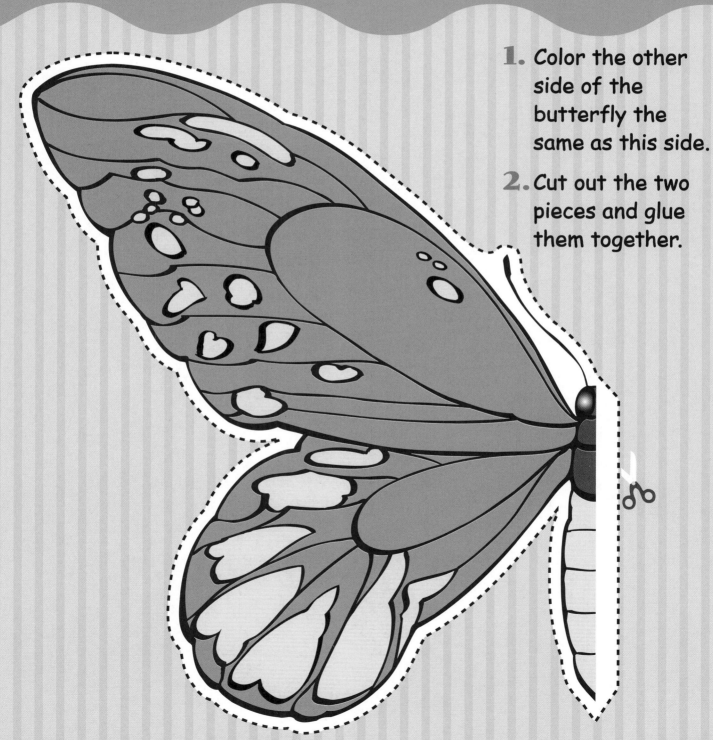

1. Color the other side of the butterfly the same as this side.
2. Cut out the two pieces and glue them together.

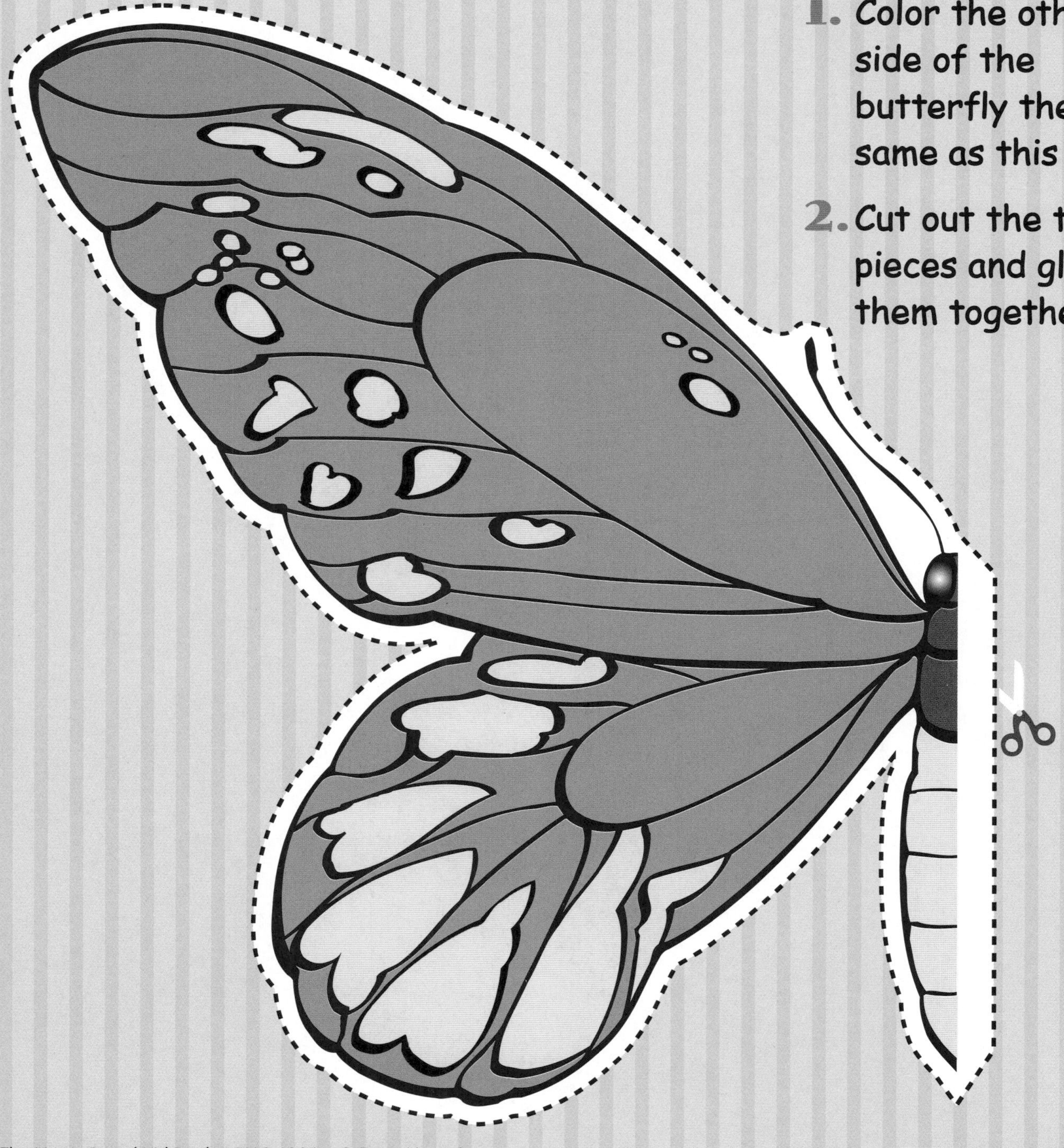

## Queen Alexandra's Birdwing Butterfly

This is the largest butterfly in the world. It has a wingspan of 12 inches (30.5 cm).

# Stag Beetle

Draw and color the other side of this stag beetle.

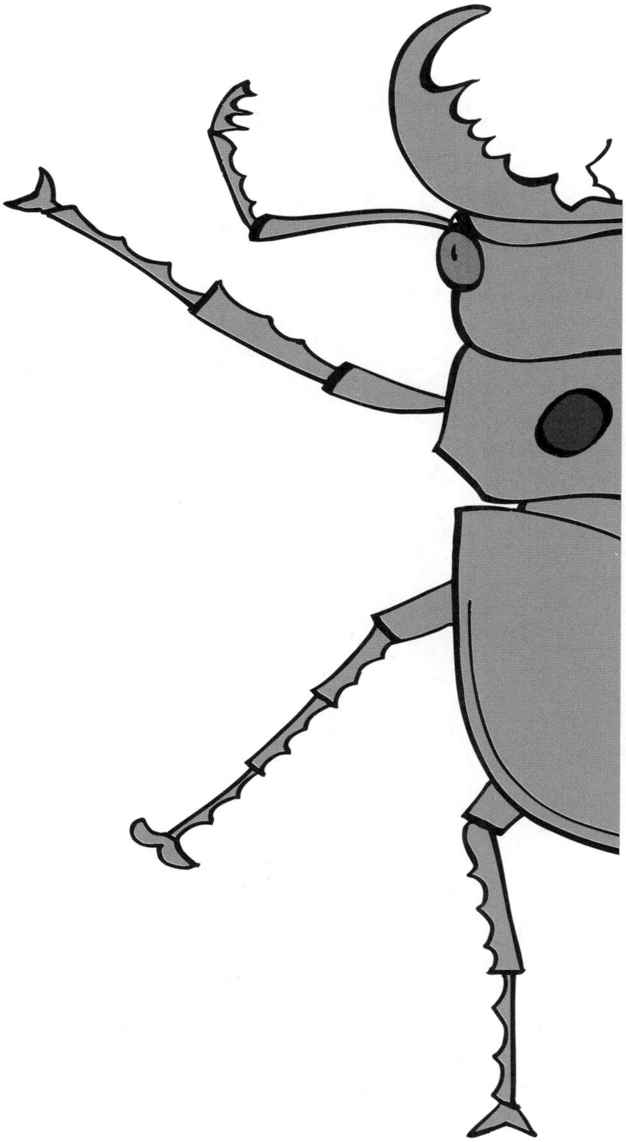

# Camouflage

Cut out the insects and match each one to the place where it can hide. This is how the insects hide from their enemies.

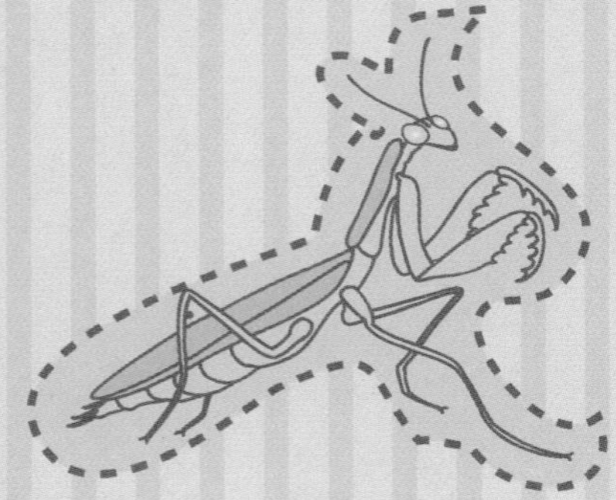

# I'm an Old Cowhand

A cowhand is a working cowboy or cowgirl. Find the words in the word search.

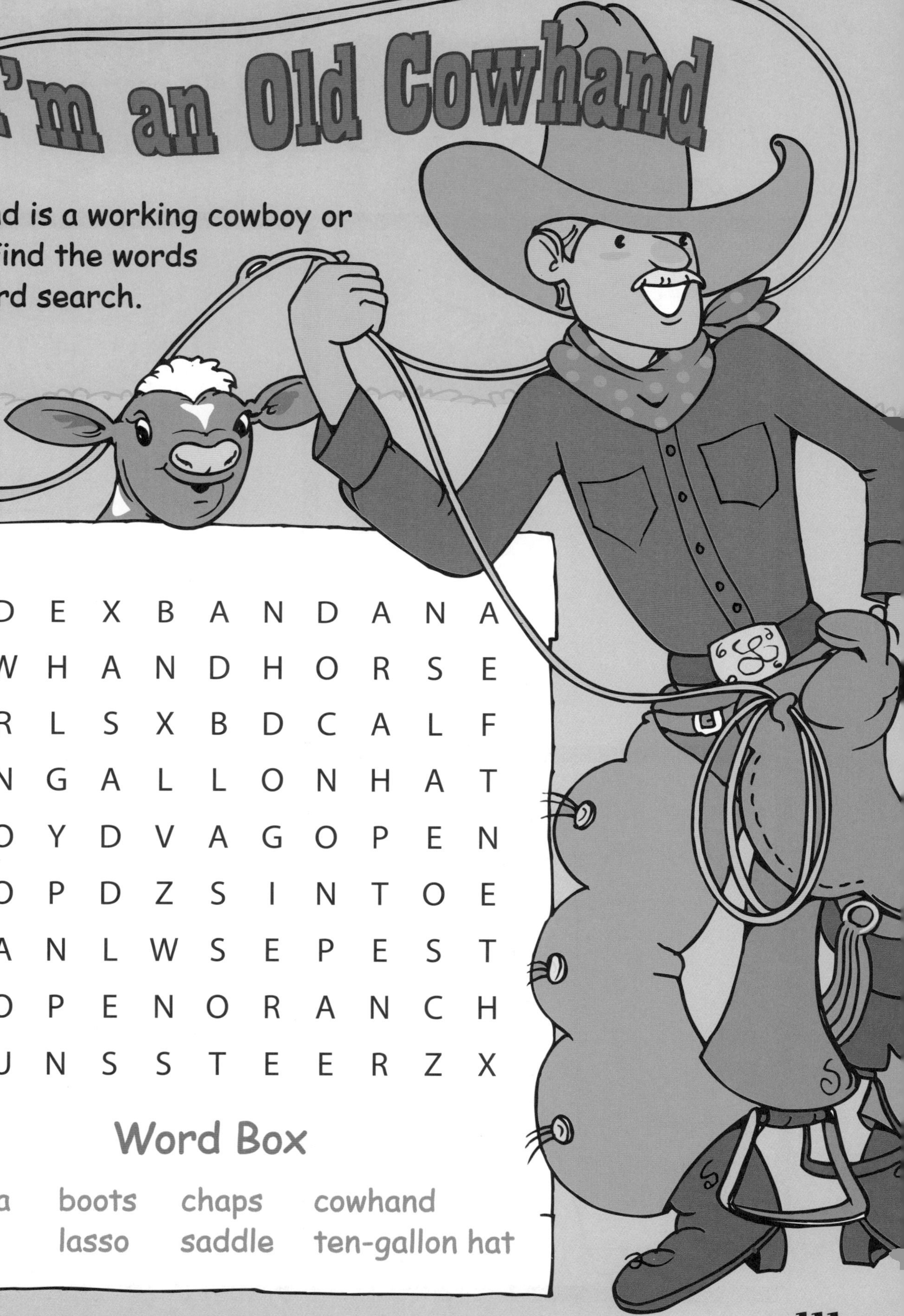

| | | | | | | | | | | | |
|---|---|---|---|---|---|---|---|---|---|---|---|
| R | I | D | E | X | B | A | N | D | A | N | A |
| C | O | W | H | A | N | D | H | O | R | S | E |
| G | I | R | L | S | X | B | D | C | A | L | F |
| T | E | N | G | A | L | L | O | N | H | A | T |
| C | B | O | Y | D | V | A | G | O | P | E | N |
| C | H | O | P | D | Z | S | I | N | T | O | E |
| V | M | A | N | L | W | S | E | P | E | S | T |
| Z | R | O | P | E | N | O | R | A | N | C | H |
| X | S | U | N | S | S | T | E | E | R | Z | X |

## Word Box

| | | | |
|---|---|---|---|
| bandana | boots | chaps | cowhand |
| dogie | lasso | saddle | ten-gallon hat |

# Draw a Cowhand

Follow these steps to draw a cowboy or cowgirl on page 113.

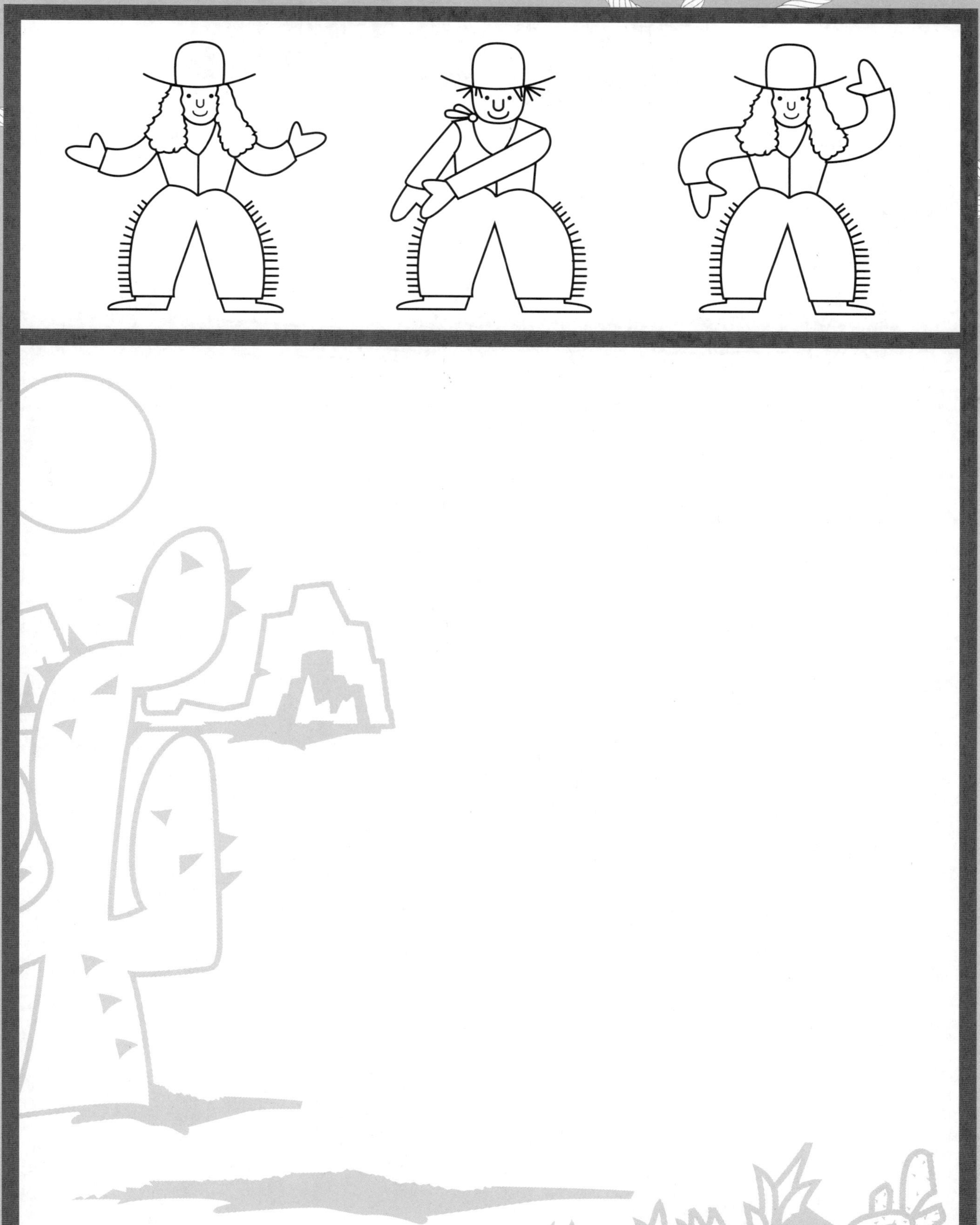

# Herd of Cattle

Help the cowhand find the two cows that are exactly alike. Circle them.

Moo
Moo
Moo
Moo
Moo
Moo
Moo
Moo

# My Horse

Read the clues. Circle my horse.

My horse has a white mark on his face.
My horse has spots.
My horse is black and white.
My horse has a black mane and tail.

Can you find him?

# What Is It?

Start at 1. Connect the dots to find the mystery animal. Color it.

1
2
3
4
5
6
7
8
9
10
11
12
13
14
15
16
17
18
19
20
21
22
23
24
25
26
27
28
29
30
31
32
33
34
35
36
37
38
39
40
41
42
43
44
45
46
47
48
49
50
51
52
53
54
55
56
57
58
59
60
61
62
63
64
65
66
67
68
69
70
71
72

# Little Lost Dogie

A dogie is a calf without a mother.
Help the cowhand find the lost dogie.

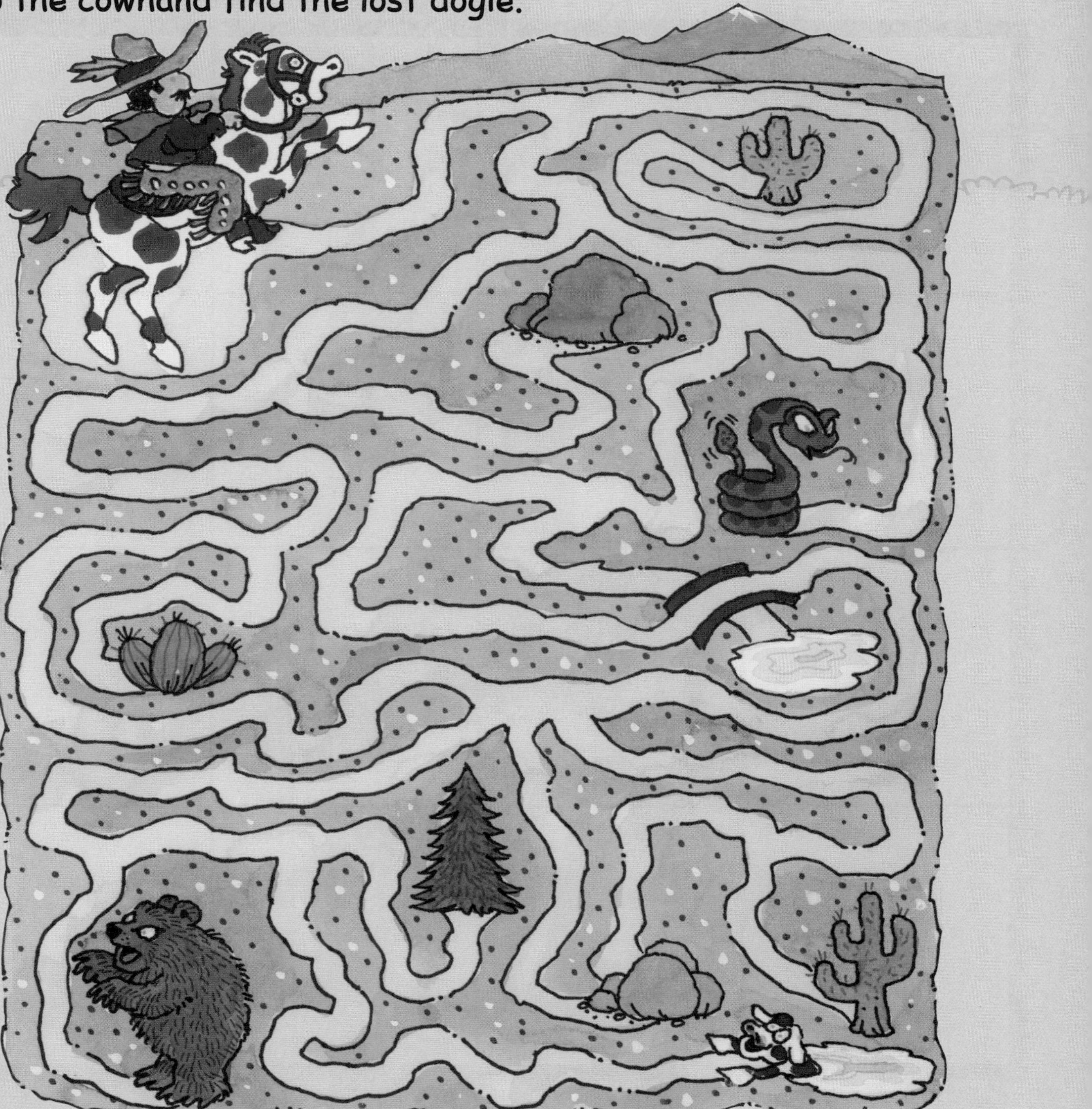

# Ride 'em, Cowboy!

Cut out the puzzle pieces on page 119.
Glue them together here.

| | | | |
|---|---|---|---|
| glue | glue | glue | glue |
| glue | glue | glue | glue |
| glue | glue | glue | glue |
| glue | glue | glue | glue |

# Cowboy Riddles

Use the code to answer the riddles.

| | | | |
|---|---|---|---|
| 1—a | 4—e | 7—m | 10—r |
| 2—b | 5—h | 8—n | 11—s |
| 3—d | 6—i | 9—o | 12—y |

What has 2 heads, 4 eyes, 6 legs, and a tail?

___   ___ ___ ___ ___ ___   ___ ___ ___
1   5 9 10 11 4   1 8 3

___ ___ ___ ___ ___
10 6 3 4 10

What does a horse have that no other animal has?

___   ___ ___ ___ ___   ___ ___ ___ ___ ___
1   2 1 2 12   5 9 10 11 4

# Cowhands Flip Book

1
Cowhands Flip Book

2
Cowhands Flip Book
Cowhands Flip Book

3

1. Remove pages 123 and 125 from the book and cut the pages apart on the dotted black lines.
2. Fold the cover and staple the pages between them.
3. Cut the red dotted lines on each page.
4. Turn the pages to make funny new characters.

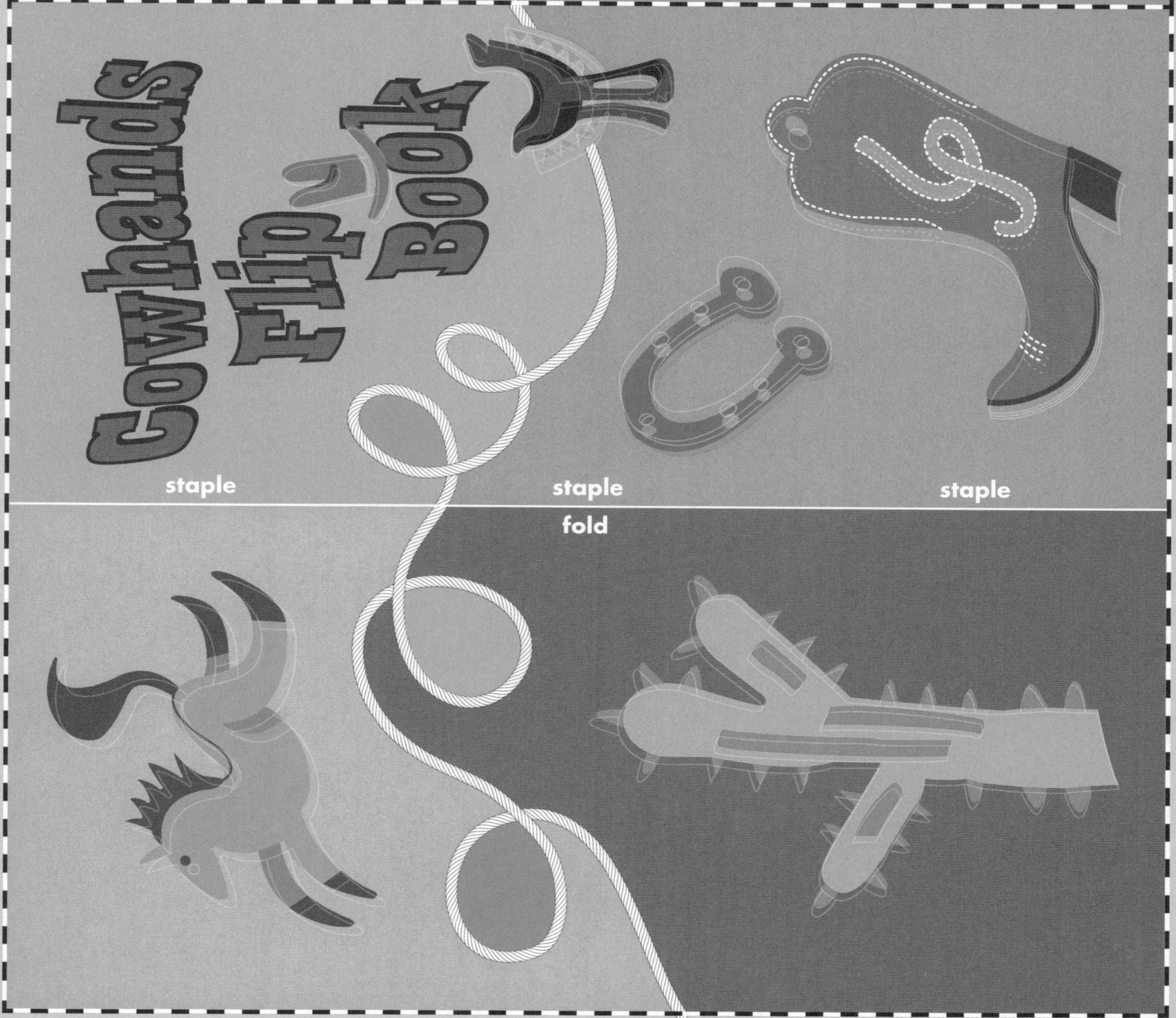
Cowhands Flip Book
staple
staple
staple
fold

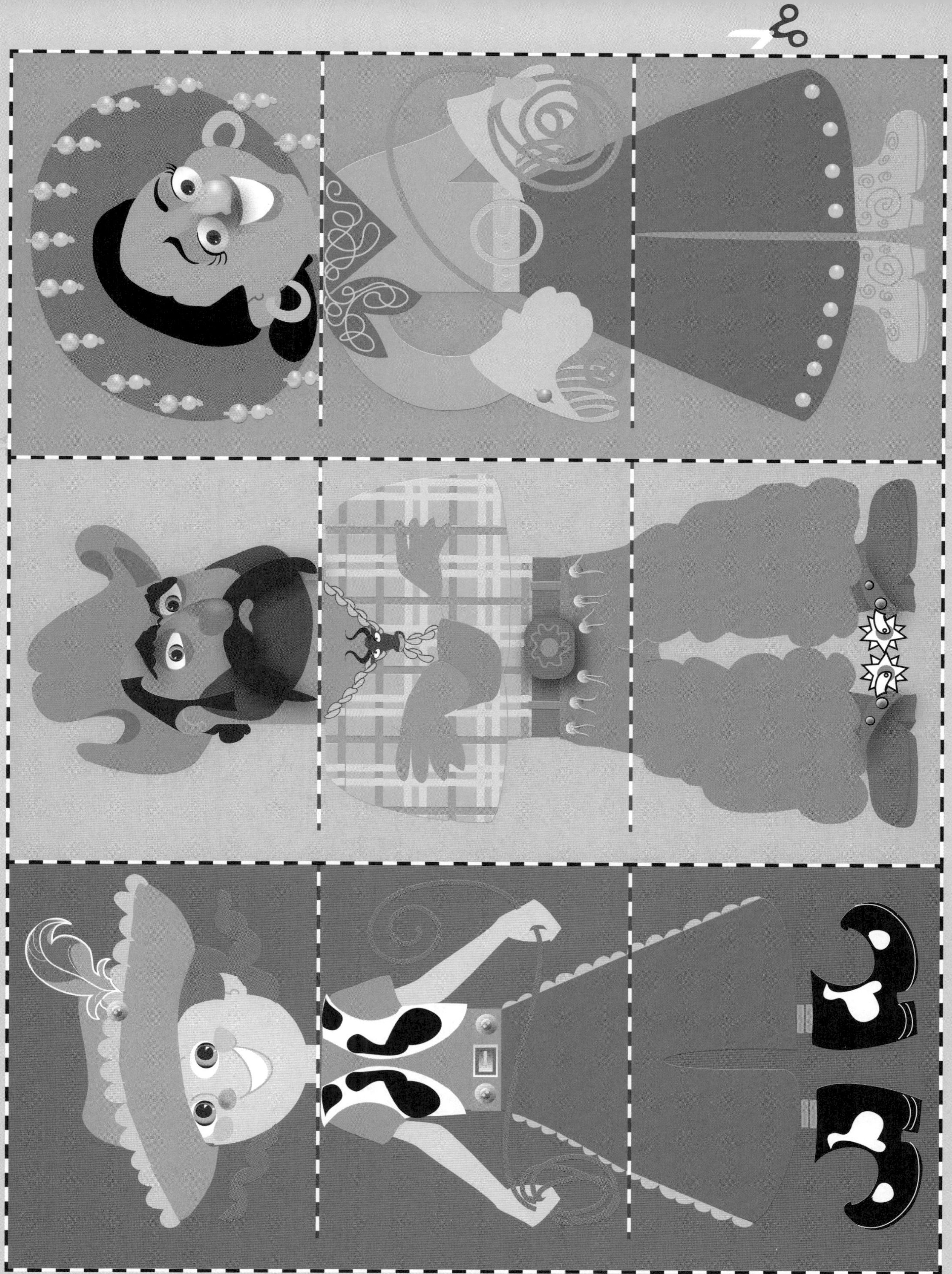

# What Is It?

Use the code to name the earth-moving equipment.

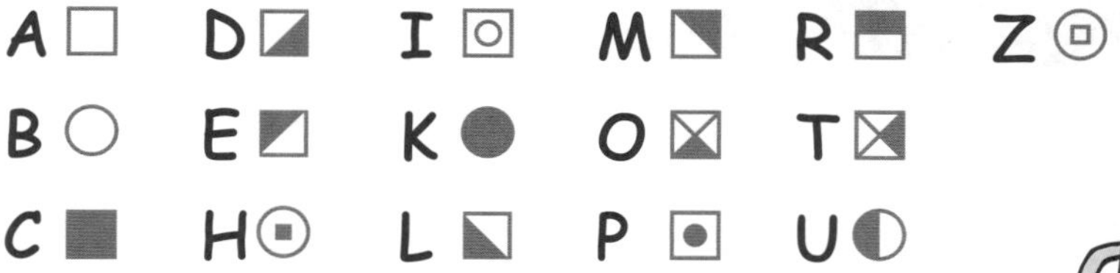

A
D
I
M
R
Z
B
E
K
O
T
C
H
L
P
U

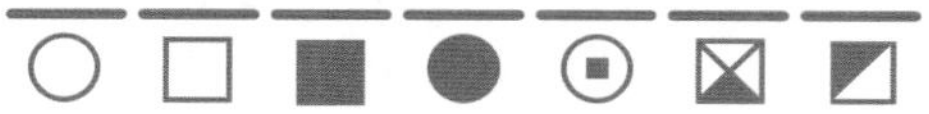

# Moving Dirt

Fill in the missing word to name the piece of equipment you would use to move the dirt.

I need to move a load of dirt to a new location.

I will use the ______________________.

I need to dig a trench for a new pipeline.

I will use the ______________________.

I need to lift dirt into the truck.

I will use the ______________________.

I need to move dirt into a pile.

I will use the ______________________.

**Word Box**

- bulldozer
- loader
- dump truck
- backhoe

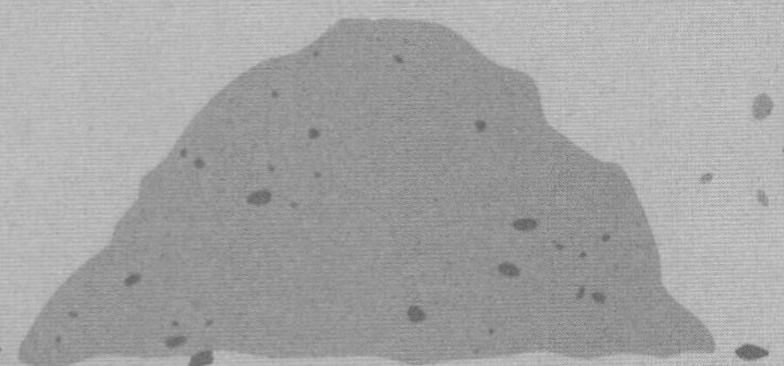

# Heavy Equipment

Circle what is wrong in this picture.

THIS SIDE
UP

# Backhoe

Start at 2. Count by 2s. Connect the dots.

2
4
6
8
10
12
14
16
18
20
22
24
26
28
30
32
34
36
38
40
42
44
46
48
50
52
54
56
58
60
62
64
66
68
70
72
74
76
78
80
82
84
86
88
90
92
94
96
98
100

# A Little Book

Remove page 131 from the book. Cut the pages apart. Staple them together in order.

staple

staple

## Flightless Birds

Flightless birds have feathers like other birds. They lay eggs like other birds. They have wings like other birds. But unlike other birds, they cannot fly.

1

cassowary
ostrich
emu

The ostrich, emu, and cassowary are very large flightless birds. Their bodies are too heavy for the size of their wings. While they cannot fly, they all run very fast with their powerful legs.

3

Penguins cannot fly, but they can swim very well. They use their wings like paddles to move them through the water.

2

The kiwi and the kakapo are small flightless birds. Their tiny wings are useless for flying, but they can run quickly.

kiwi
kakapo

4

# Flightless Birds

Find these flightless birds in the word search.

kiwi

kakapo

| | | | | | | | | | |
|---|---|---|---|---|---|---|---|---|---|
| L | K | W | P | E | N | G | U | I | N |
| E | B | I | G | Z | M | X | F | A | R |
| G | N | U | W | O | D | U | C | K | A |
| O | S | T | R | I | C | H | T | E | N |
| O | C | A | S | S | O | W | A | R | Y |
| S | W | I | M | K | A | K | A | P | O |

ostrich

cassowary

emu

penguin

# What Am I?

Start at 2. Count by 2s to connect the dots. Color the picture.

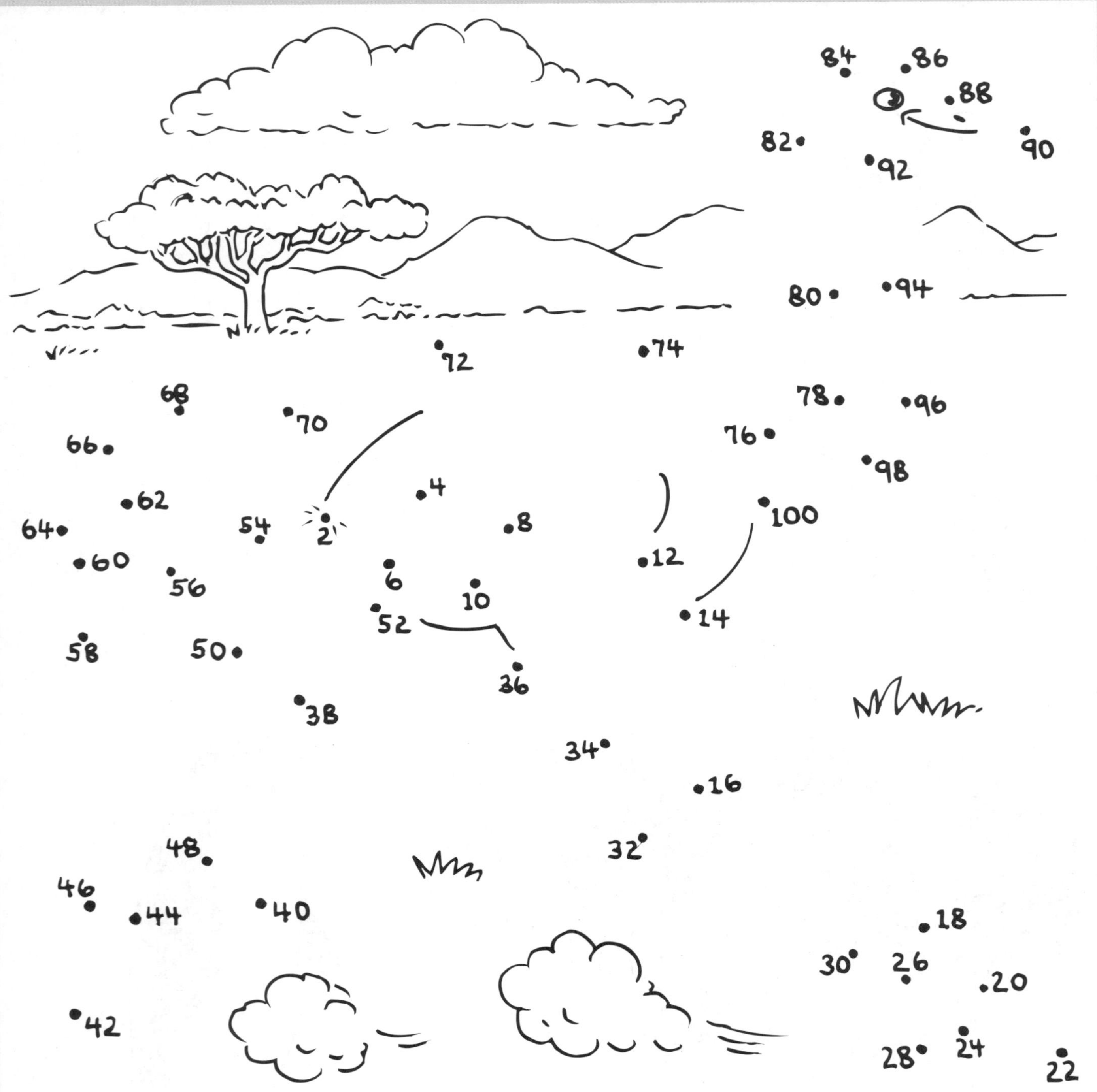

84
86
88
82
90
92
80
94
72
74
68
78
96
70
66
76
98
4
62
54
8
100
64
2
60
12
56
6
10
52
14
58
50
36
38
34
16
48
32
46
44
40
18
30
26
20
42
28
24
22


Circle the name of the bird you made.

penguin ostrich kiwi

# Kakapo

Color the kakapo.
It is shades of green and brown.

The kakapo is a flightless parrot. It lives in New Zealand. It is a nocturnal bird. This means that it is most active at night. It cannot fly, but it uses its wings to glide from tree to tree. It uses its strong legs to climb tall trees.

# Penguin

Draw and color this penguin on page 137.

Penguins are flightless seabirds. They use their wings underwater as powerful flippers. Their bodies are covered by three layers of short feathers to keep them warm. These birds eat mostly fish and squid.

# Riddle Time

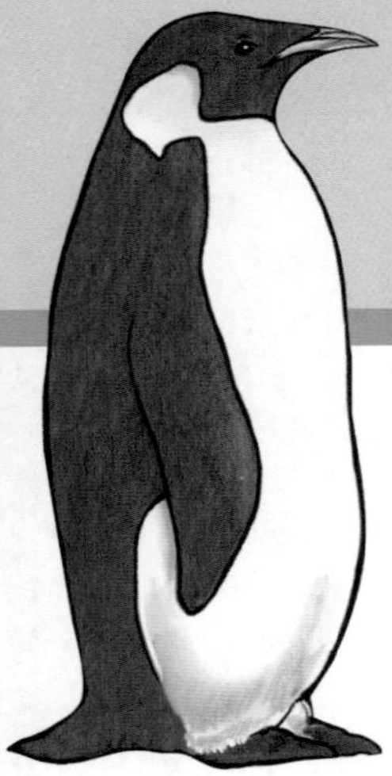

Use the code to help you answer the riddles.

| | | | | | |
|---|---|---|---|---|---|
| 1—a | 4—e | 7—h | 10—n | 13—r | 16—u |
| 2—c | 5—f | 8—i | 11—o | 14—s | 17—v |
| 3—d | 6—g | 9—k | 12—p | 15—t | 18—y |

Why do penguins carry fish in their beaks?

15 7 4 18   3 11 10 ' 15

7 1 17 4   12 11 2 9 4 15 14

Why do ostriches have such long legs?

14 11   15 7 4 8 13

5 4 4 15   2 1 10

15 11 16 2 7   15 7 4

6 13 11 16 10 3

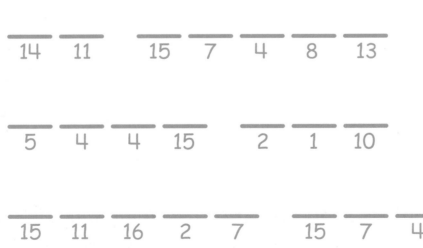

# Where Are My Babies?

Mother Ostrich has lost her babies. She needs your help to find them. Color the babies as you find them in this picture.

How many babies did you find in all?

# Name the Birds

Write the name of each flightless bird on the lines.

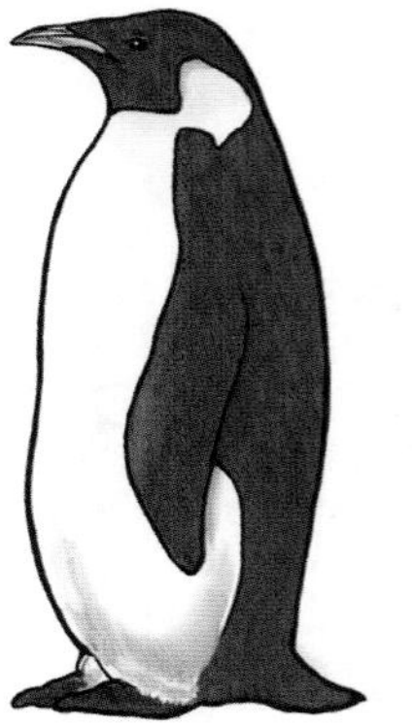

## Word Box

ostrich emu kiwi cassowary penguin kakapo

# Bread Search

How many times can you find bread in the puzzle?

| | | | | | | | | | | | |
|---|---|---|---|---|---|---|---|---|---|---|---|
| J | A | M | B | R | E | A | D | M | I | L | K |
| B | R | E | A | D | B | T | N | A | A | N | B |
| Z | L | O | A | F | R | O | B | T | P | C | R |
| R | O | S | L | I | E | R | I | Z | P | R | E |
| Y | B | A | G | L | A | T | N | O | L | A | A |
| E | P | I | T | A | D | I | G | E | S | C | D |
| B | R | E | A | D | S | L | I | C | E | K | X |
| M | U | F | F | I | N | L | B | A | G | E | L |
| S | U | N | B | R | E | A | D | O | O | R | D |

Now find these kinds of bread.

| | | | |
|---|---|---|---|
| bagel | matzo | roll | loaf |
| bun | naan | rye | muffin |
| cracker | pita | slice | tortilla |

# All Kinds of Bread

Cut out the puzzle pieces on page 143.
Glue them together here.

| | | | |
|---|---|---|---|
| glue | glue | glue | glue |
| glue | glue | glue | glue |
| glue | glue | glue | glue |
| glue | glue | glue | glue |

# Mystery Fish

Start at 1. Connect the dots to find the mystery fish.

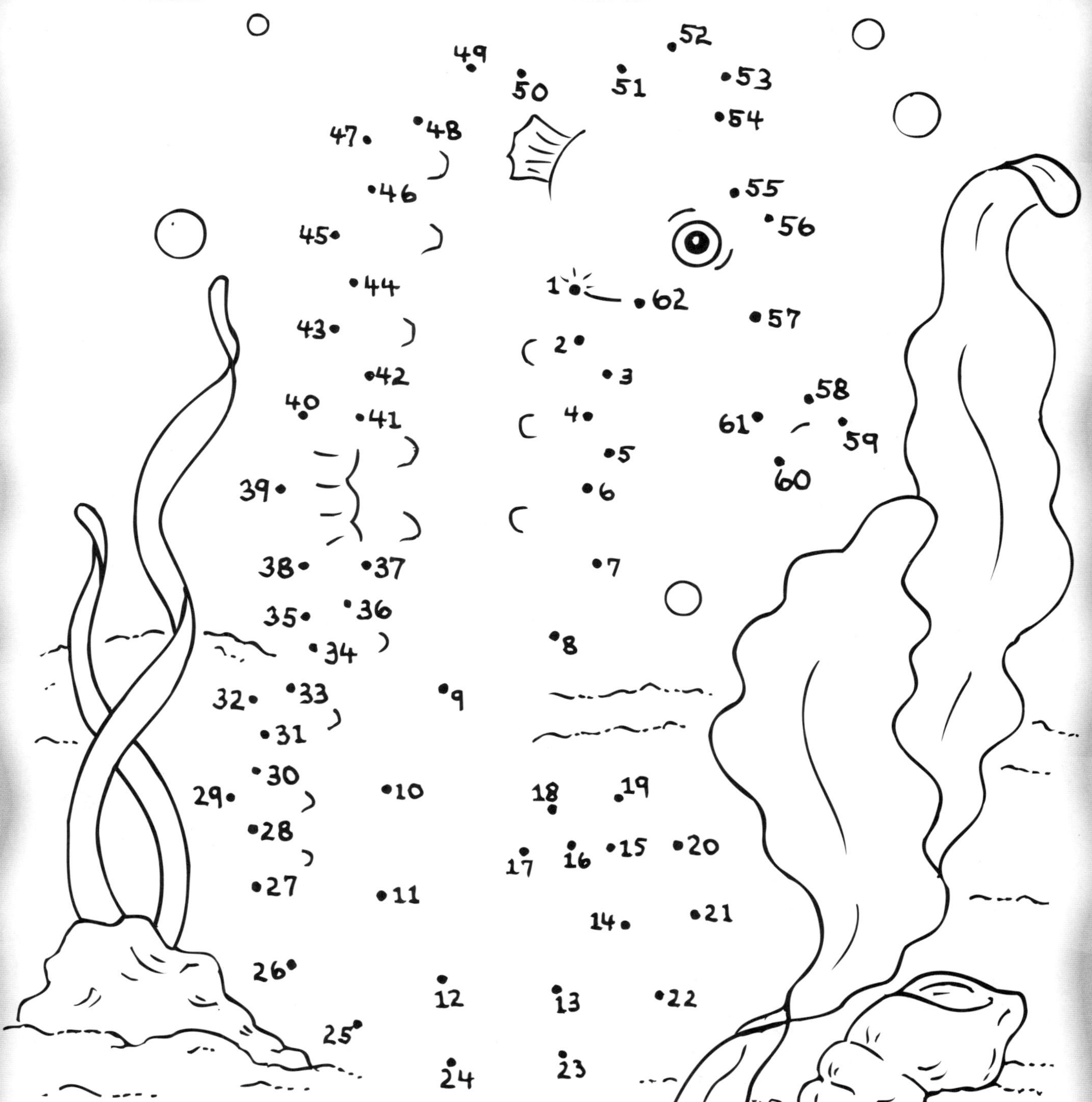

# Did You Know...?

- A sea horse is a kind of fish.
- Most sea horses are small, but the Pacific sea horse can be as big as 1 foot (30.5 cm) in length.
- A sea horse has a prehensile tail. This means it can use its tail to hold on to plants such as sea grasses.
- A sea horse's color matches its surroundings. This helps the sea horse hide from its enemies.
- The male sea horse has a pouch. He carries eggs in his pouch until they hatch. He can carry as many as 100 eggs at a time.

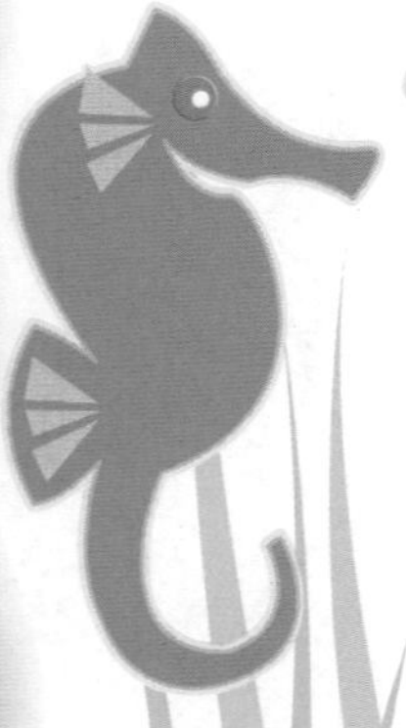

# Name the Parts

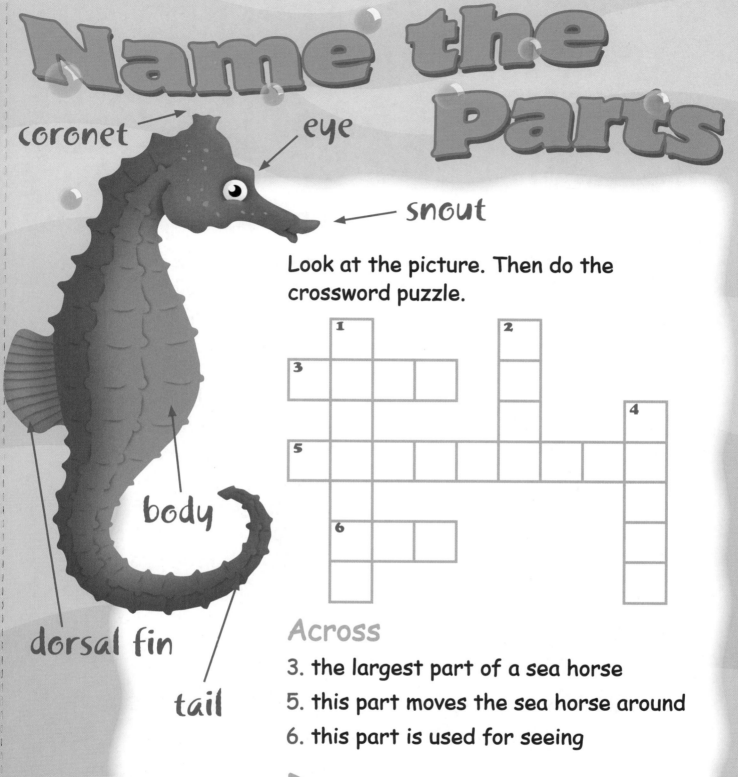

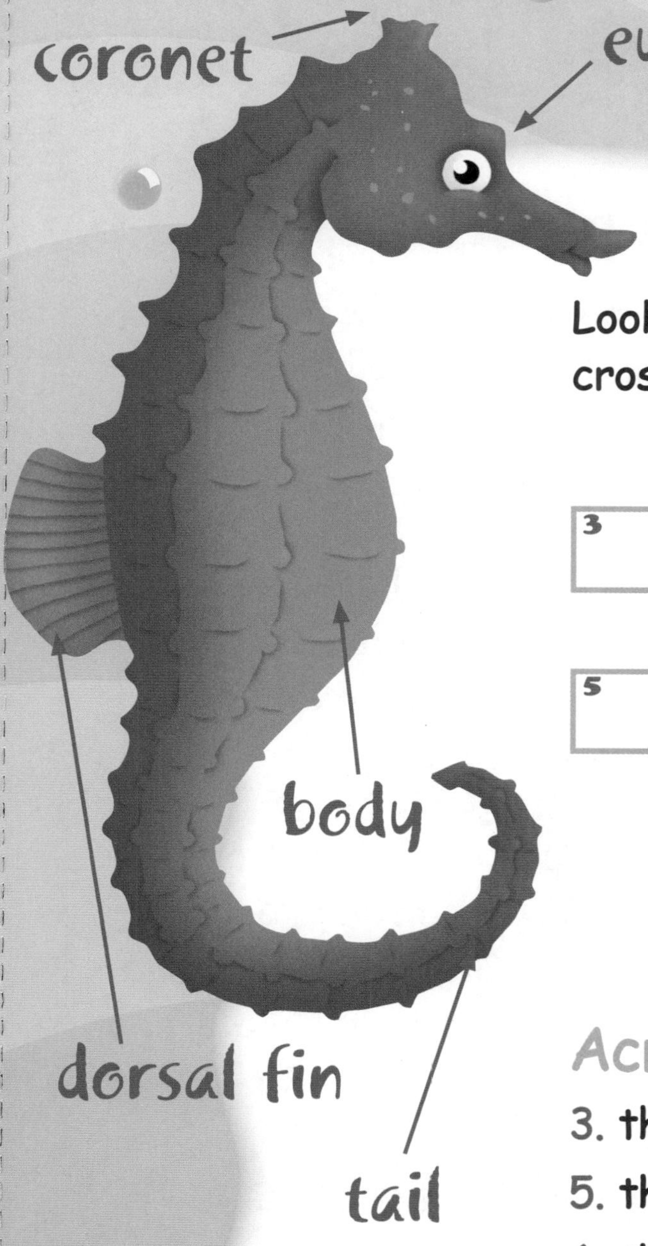
coronet
eye
snout
body
dorsal fin
tail

Look at the picture. Then do the crossword puzzle.

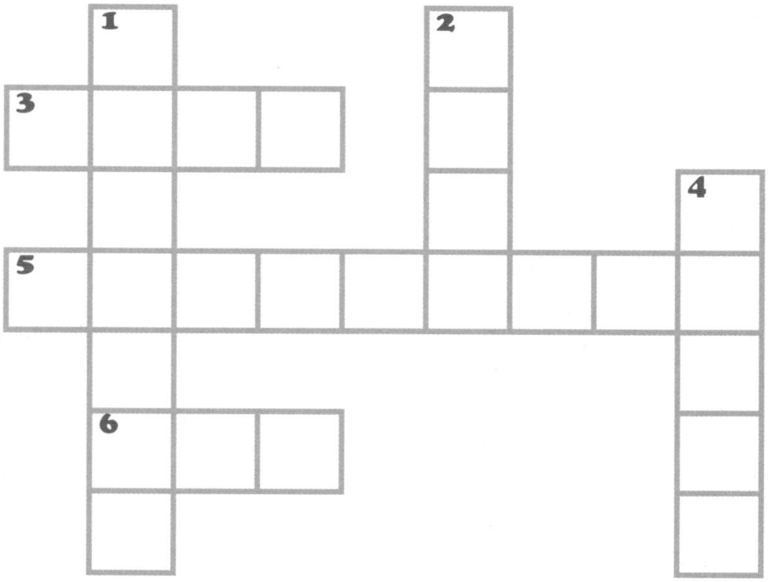
1
2
3
4
5
6

## Across

3. the largest part of a sea horse
5. this part moves the sea horse around
6. this part is used for seeing

## Down

1. the top of the sea horse's head
2. this part can curl around sea grass
4. the nose and mouth part of a sea horse

# Leafy Sea Dragon

## A Pop-up Card

1. Remove page 149 from the book. Cut out the leafy sea dragon and the pop-up form. Fold the form in half.

2. Cut the tabs. Fold and crease the tabs in both directions. Open the form and pull the tabs forward.

3. Put glue on the front of the tab. Glue the sea dragon to the tab. Open and close the form to watch the sea dragon pop up.

1
fold
cut
cut

2
cut
cut

3
glue
fold
GLUE

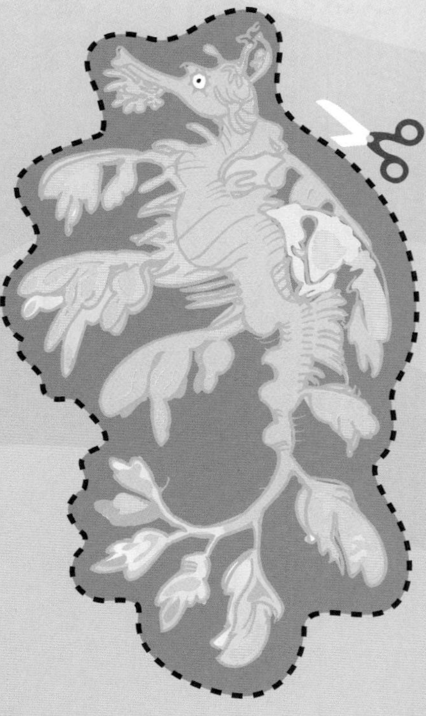

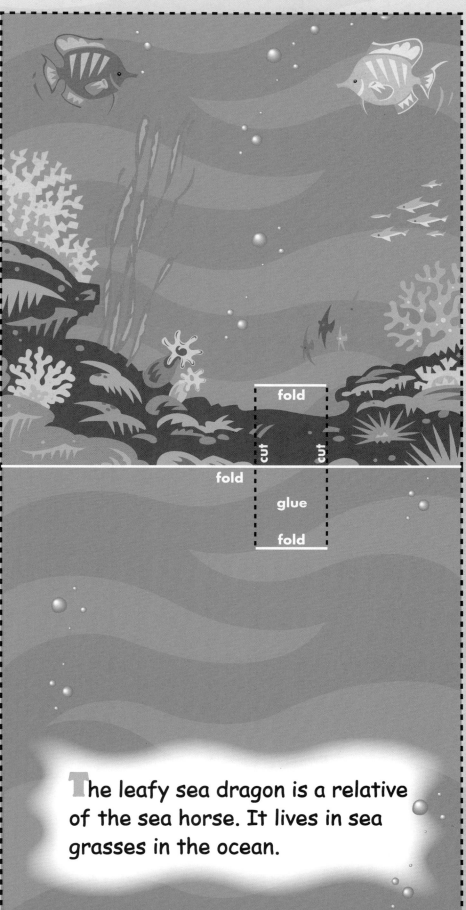

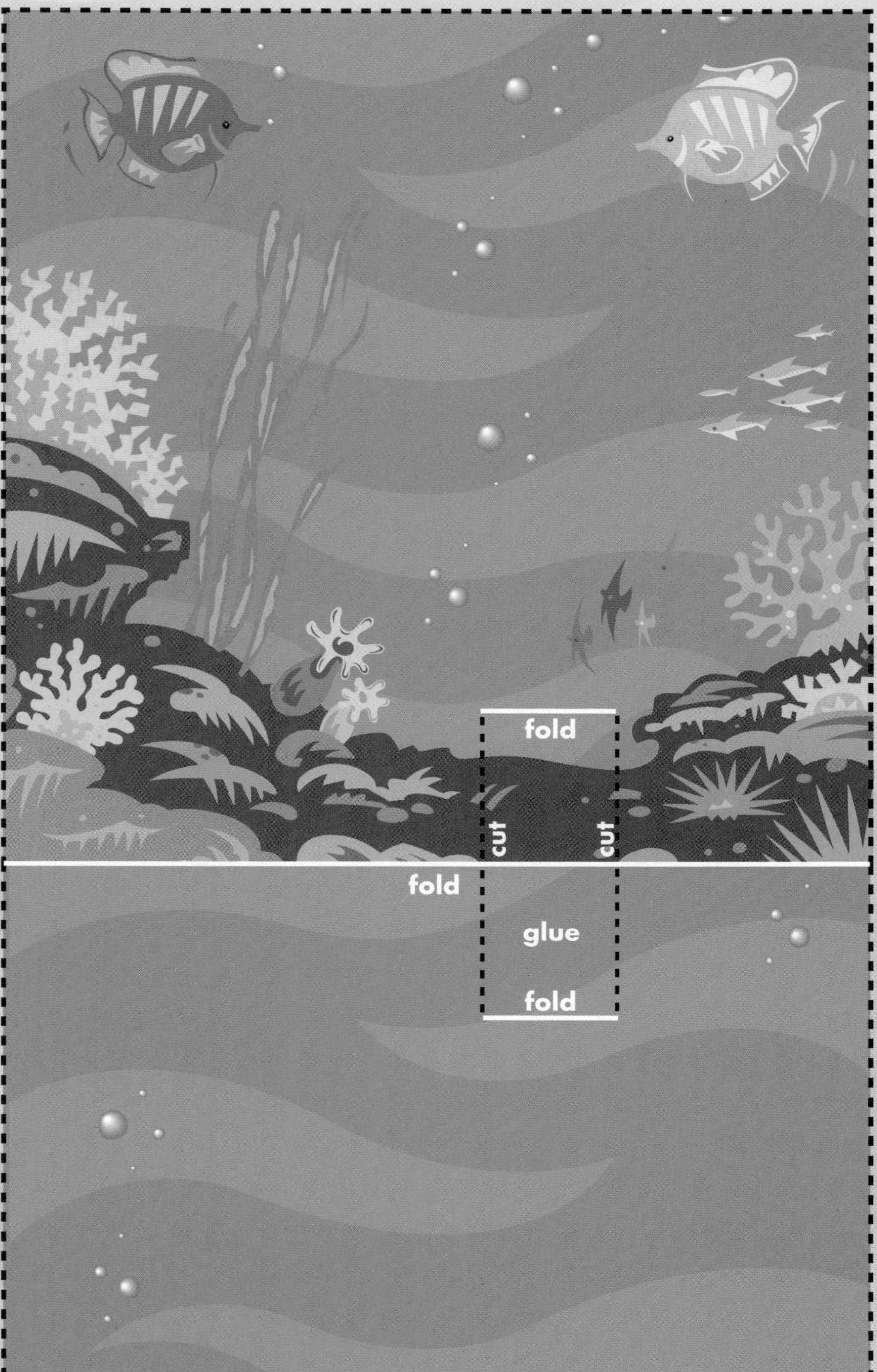
fold
cut
cut
fold
glue
fold

The leafy sea dragon is a relative of the sea horse. It lives in sea grasses in the ocean.

Leafy

Sea

Dragon

# Hammerhead Shark

The hammerhead shark is another unusual fish found in Earth's oceans.

Draw and color the other side of this hammerhead shark.

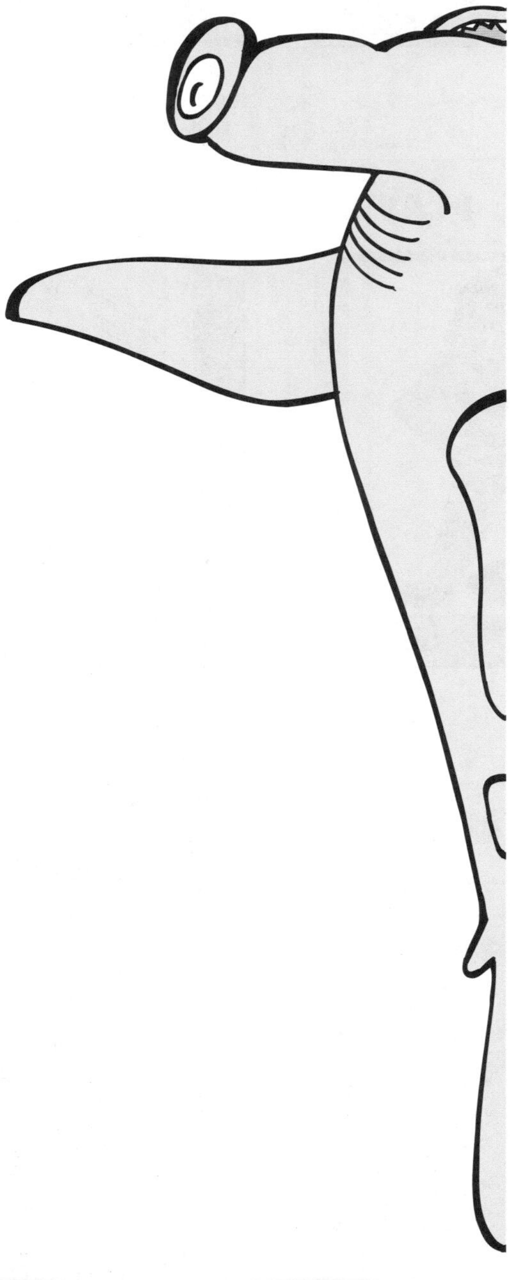

# Answer Key

## Page 4

PLAY BALL!
Find the names of all the ball games.
Word Box
badminton croquet pool baseball cricket
football rugby basketball golf ping-pong
soccer bowling hockey tennis volleyball
4
The Never-Bored Kid Book • EMC 6304 • © Evan-Moor Corp.

## Page 5

LOST BALLS
Coach is unhappy. All of the balls are lost.
See how many you can find. Color them.
The Never-Bored Kid Book • EMC 6304 • © Evan-Moor Corp.
5

## Page 6

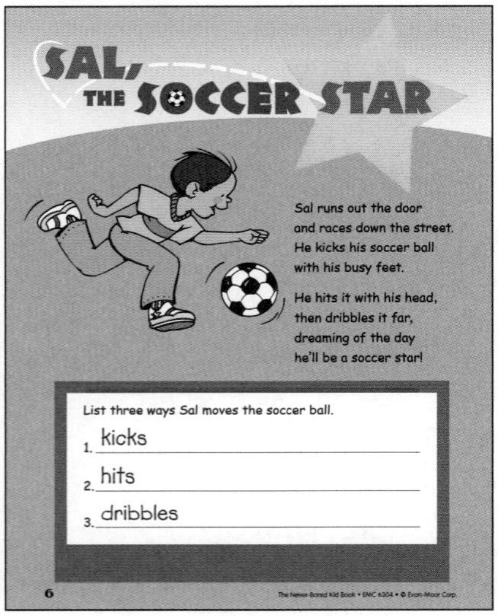
SAL, THE SOCCER STAR
Sal runs out the door
and races down the street.
He kicks his soccer ball
with his busy feet.
He hits it with his head,
then dribbles it far,
dreaming of the day
he'll be a soccer star!
List three ways Sal moves the soccer ball.
1. kicks
2. hits
3. dribbles
6
The Never-Bored Kid Book • EMC 6304 • © Evan-Moor Corp.

## Page 7

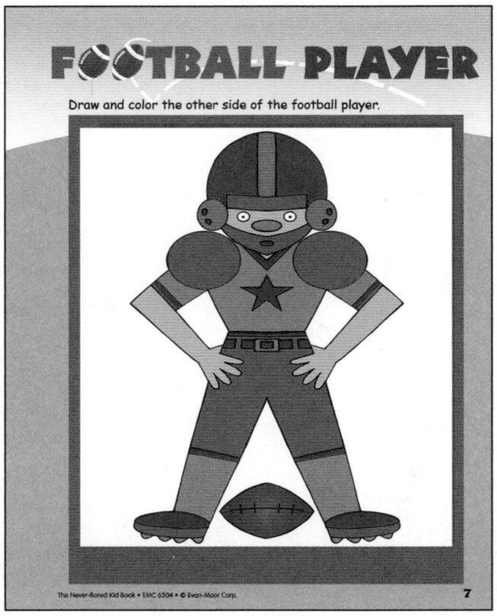
FOOTBALL PLAYER
Draw and color the other side of the football player.
The Never-Bored Kid Book • EMC 6304 • © Evan-Moor Corp.
7

## Page 8

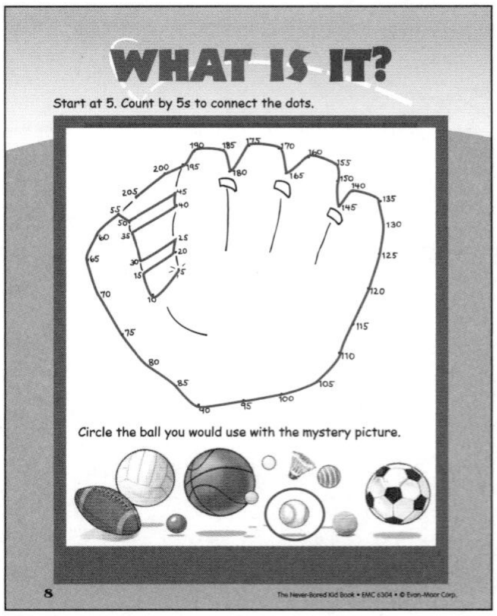
WHAT IS IT?
Start at 5. Count by 5s to connect the dots.
Circle the ball you would use with the mystery picture.
8
The Never-Bored Kid Book • EMC 6304 • © Evan-Moor Corp.

## Page 9

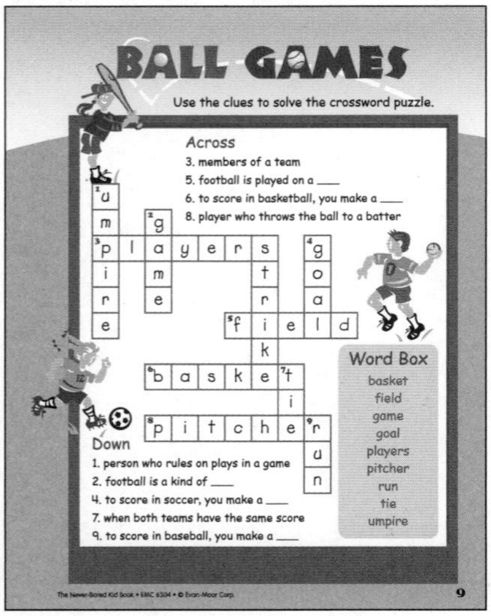
BALL GAMES
Use the clues to solve the crossword puzzle.
Across
3. members of a team
5. football is played on a ___
6. to score in basketball, you make a ___
8. player who throws the ball to a batter
Down
1. person who rules on plays in a game
2. football is a kind of ___
4. to score in soccer, you make a ___
7. when both teams have the same score
9. to score in baseball, you make a ___
Word Box
basket
field
game
goal
players
pitcher
run
tie
umpire
The Never-Bored Kid Book • EMC 6304 • © Evan-Moor Corp.
9

## Page 10

GO FOR A GOAL
Help the soccer player make a goal.
10
The Never-Bored Kid Book • EMC 6304 • © Evan-Moor Corp.

## Page 11

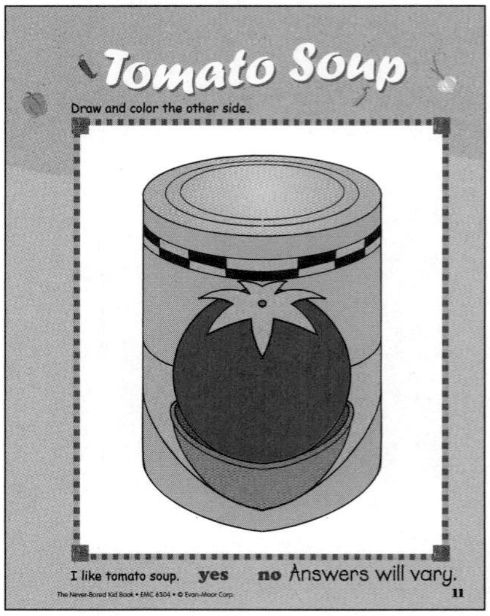
Tomato Soup
Draw and color the other side.
I like tomato soup. yes no Answers will vary.
The Never-Bored Kid Book • EMC 6304 • © Evan-Moor Corp.
11

## Page 14

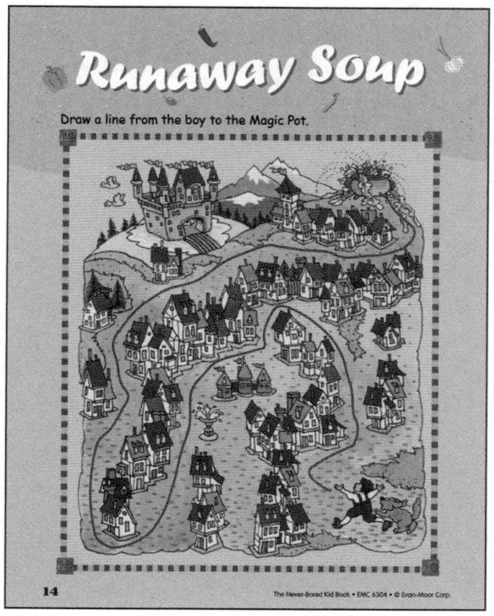
Runaway Soup
Draw a line from the boy to the Magic Pot.
14
The Never-Bored Kid Book • EMC 6304 • © Evan-Moor Corp.

## Page 15

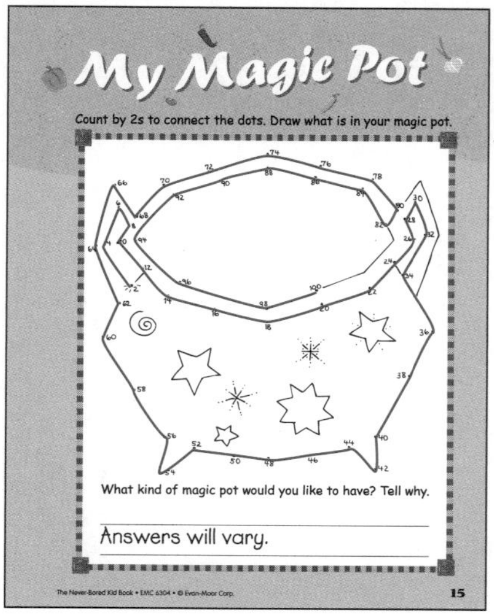
My Magic Pot
Count by 2s to connect the dots. Draw what is in your magic pot.
What kind of magic pot would you like to have? Tell why.
Answers will vary.
The Never-Bored Kid Book • EMC 6304 • © Evan-Moor Corp.
15

## Page 16

Vegetable Soup
Find the vegetables in the soup pot.
Word Box
beans
carrot
celery
garlic
onion
parsnip
peas
potatoes
rutabaga
spinach
turnip
yam
16
The Never-Bored Kid Book • EMC 6304 • © Evan-Moor Corp.

## Page 17

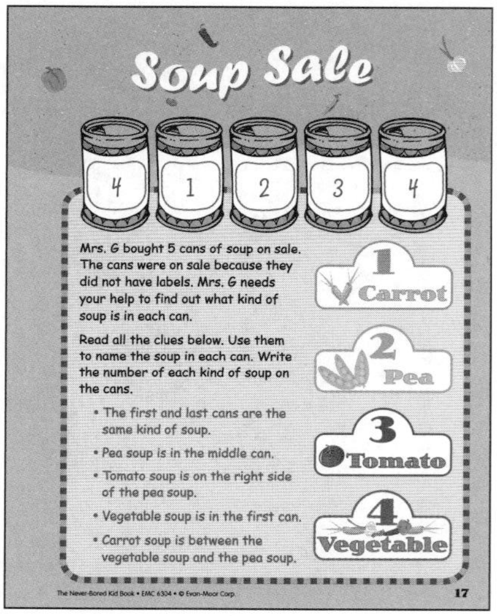
Soup Sale
4 1 2 3 4
Mrs. G bought 5 cans of soup on sale. The cans were on sale because they did not have labels. Mrs. G needs your help to find out what kind of soup is in each can.
Read all the clues below. Use them to name the soup in each can. Write the number of each kind of soup on the cans.
• The first and last cans are the same kind of soup.
• Pea soup is in the middle can.
• Tomato soup is on the right side of the pea soup.
• Vegetable soup is in the first can.
• Carrot soup is between the vegetable soup and the pea soup.
1 Carrot
2 Pea
3 Tomato
4 Vegetable
The Never-Bored Kid Book • EMC 6304 • © Evan-Moor Corp.
17

## Page 18

A Limerick
There was a young lady whose bonnet
Came untied when the birds sat upon it.
But she said, "I don't care!
All the birds of the air
Are welcome to sit on my bonnet."
How many birds are on the lady's bonnet? 5
18
The Never-Bored Kid Book • EMC 6304 • © Evan-Moor Corp.

## Page 19

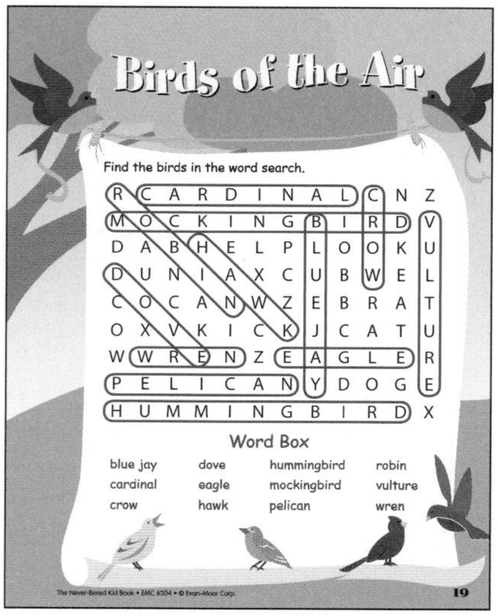
Birds of the Air
Find the birds in the word search.
Word Box
blue jay
cardinal
crow
dove
eagle
hawk
hummingbird
mockingbird
pelican
robin
vulture
wren
The Never-Bored Kid Book • EMC 6304 • © Evan-Moor Corp.
19

## Page 20

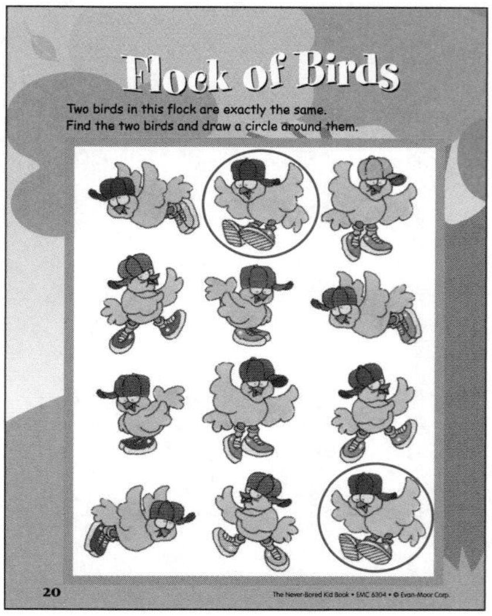
Flock of Birds
Two birds in this flock are exactly the same.
Find the two birds and draw a circle around them.
20
The Never-Bored Kid Book • EMC 6304 • © Evan-Moor Corp.

## Page 23

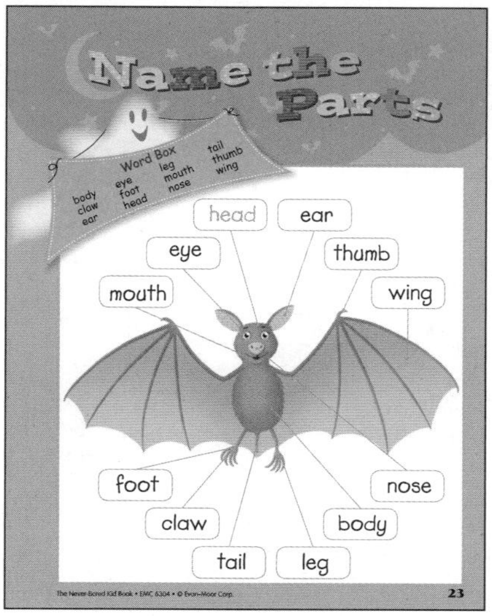
Name the Parts
Word Box
body
claw
ear
eye
foot
head
leg
mouth
nose
tail
thumb
wing
head
ear
eye
thumb
mouth
wing
foot
nose
claw
body
tail
leg
The Never-Bored Kid Book • EMC 6304 • © Evan-Moor Corp.
23

## Page 25

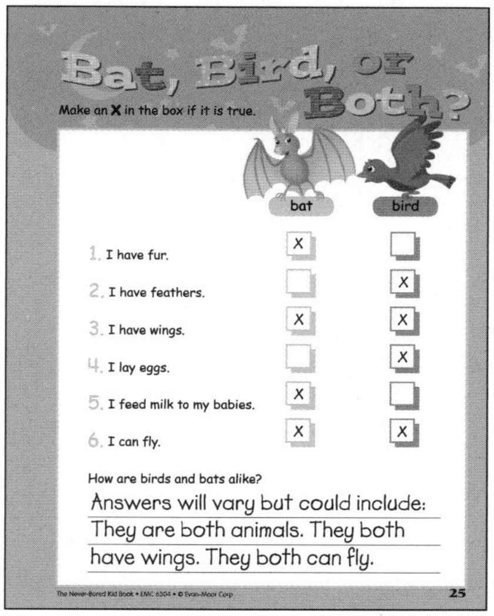
Bat, Bird, or Both?
Make an X in the box if it is true.
bat
bird
1. I have fur. X
2. I have feathers. X
3. I have wings. X X
4. I lay eggs. X
5. I feed milk to my babies. X
6. I can fly. X X
How are birds and bats alike?
Answers will vary but could include:
They are both animals. They both
have wings. They both can fly.
The Never-Bored Kid Book • EMC 6304 • © Evan-Moor Corp.
25

## Page 26

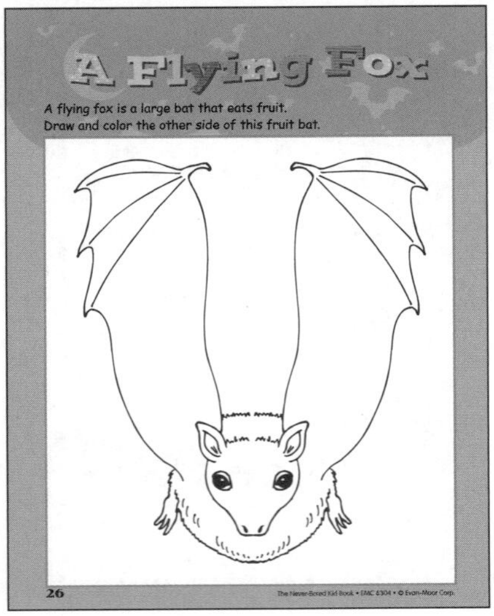
A Flying Fox
A flying fox is a large bat that eats fruit.
Draw and color the other side of this fruit bat.
26
The Never-Bored Kid Book • EMC 6304 • © Evan-Moor Corp.

## Page 27

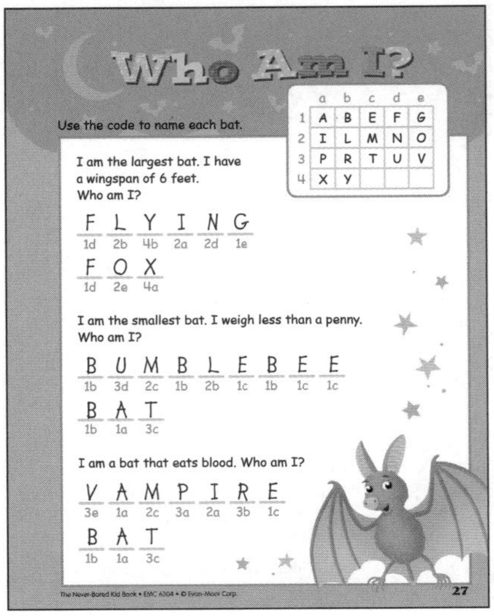
Who Am I?
Use the code to name each bat.
a b c d e
1 A B E F G
2 I L M N O
3 P R T U V
4 X Y
I am the largest bat. I have a wingspan of 6 feet. Who am I?
F L Y I N G
1d 2b 4b 2a 2d 1e
F O X
1d 2e 4a
I am the smallest bat. I weigh less than a penny. Who am I?
B U M B L E B E E
1b 3d 2c 1b 2b 1c 1b 1c 1c
B A T
1b 1a 3c
I am a bat that eats blood. Who am I?
V A M P I R E
3e 1a 2c 3a 2a 3b 1c
B A T
1b 1a 3c
The Never-Bored Kid Book • EMC 6304 • © Evan-Moor Corp.
27

## Page 28

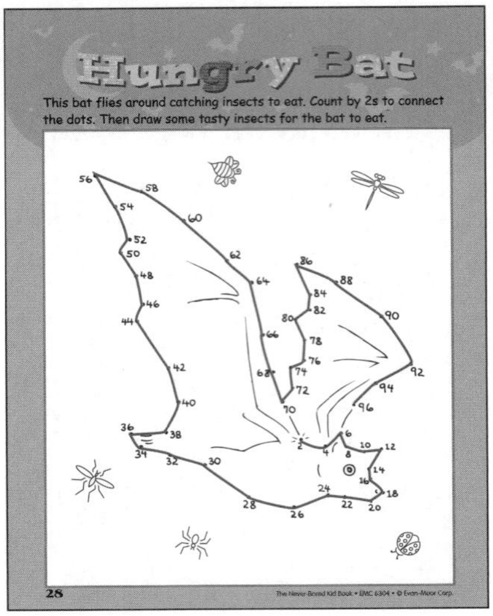
Hungry Bat
This bat flies around catching insects to eat. Count by 2s to connect the dots. Then draw some tasty insects for the bat to eat.
28
The Never-Bored Kid Book • EMC 6304 • © Evan-Moor Corp.

## Page 29

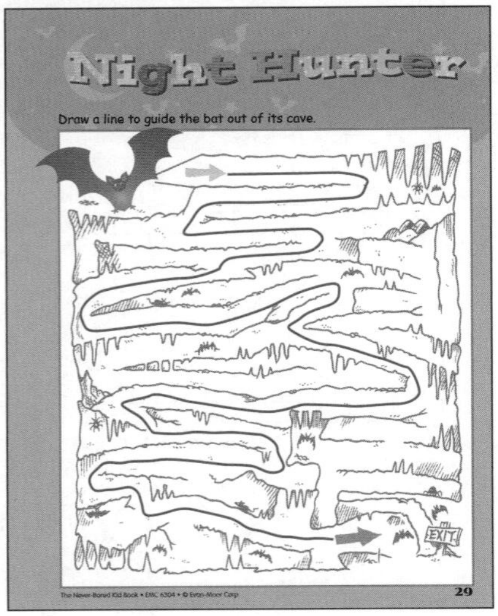
Night Hunter
Draw a line to guide the bat out of its cave.
EXIT
The Never-Bored Kid Book • EMC 6304 • © Evan-Moor Corp.
29

## Page 37

At the Races
The Never-Bored Kid Book • EMC 6304 • © Evan-Moor Corp.
37

## Page 39

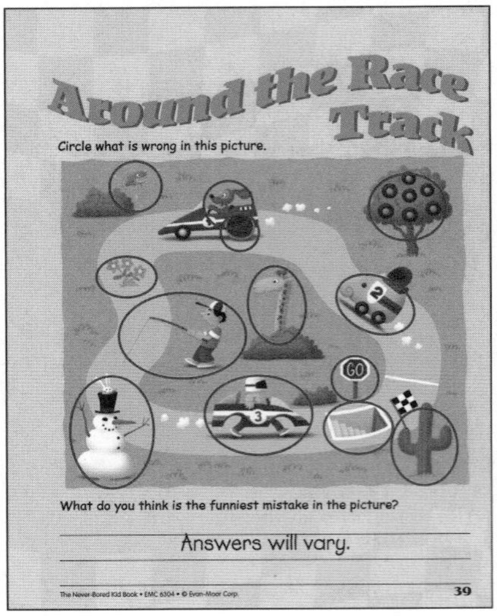
Around the Race Track
Circle what is wrong in this picture.
What do you think is the funniest mistake in the picture?
Answers will vary.
The Never-Bored Kid Book • EMC 6304 • © Evan-Moor Corp.
39

## Page 40

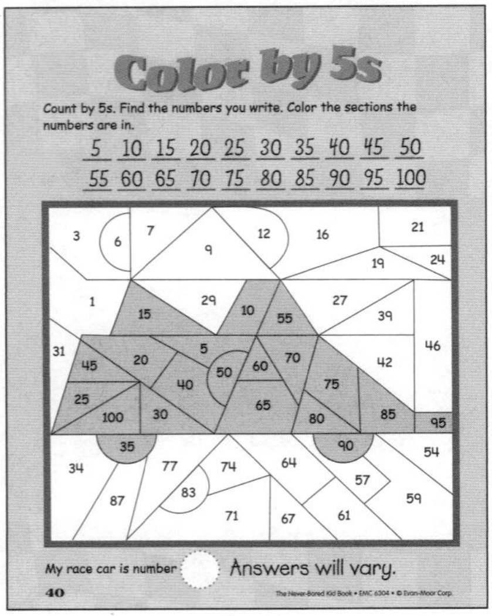
Color by 5s
Count by 5s. Find the numbers you write. Color the sections the numbers are in.
5 10 15 20 25 30 35 40 45 50
55 60 65 70 75 80 85 90 95 100
My race car is number Answers will vary.
40
The Never-Bored Kid Book • EMC 6304 • © Evan-Moor Corp.

## Page 47

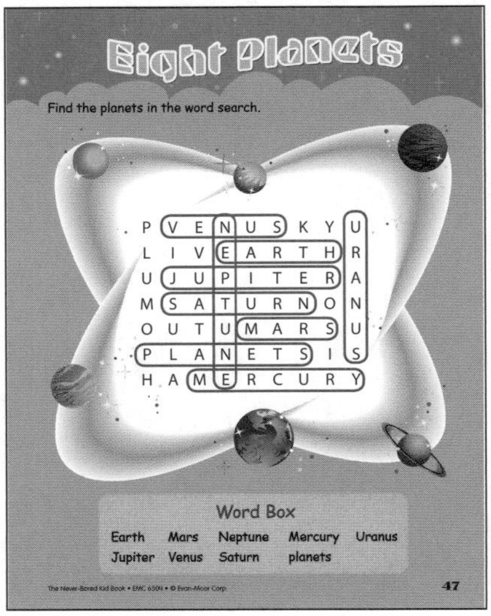
Eight Planets
Find the planets in the word search.
P V E N U S K Y U
L I V E A R T H R
U J U P I T E R A
M S A T U R N O N
O U T U M A R S U
P L A N E T S I S
H A M E R C U R Y
Word Box
Earth Mars Neptune Mercury Uranus
Jupiter Venus Saturn planets
The Never-Bored Kid Book • EMC 6304 • © Evan-Moor Corp.
47

## Page 48

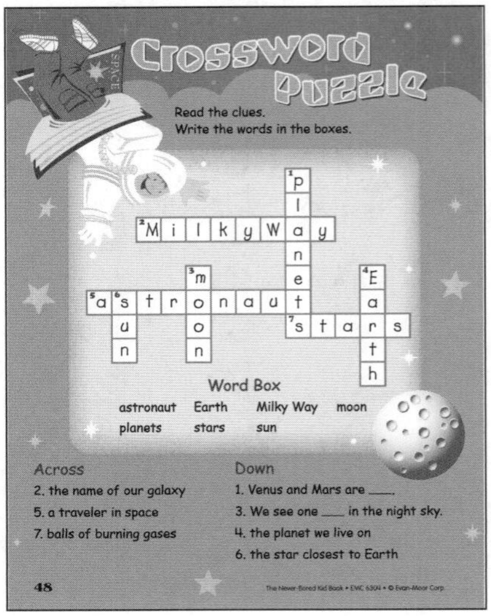
Crossword Puzzle
Read the clues.
Write the words in the boxes.
Word Box
astronaut Earth Milky Way moon
planets stars sun
Across
2. the name of our galaxy
5. a traveler in space
7. balls of burning gases
Down
1. Venus and Mars are ___.
3. We see one ___ in the night sky.
4. the planet we live on
6. the star closest to Earth
48
The Never-Bored Kid Book • EMC 6304 • © Evan-Moor Corp.

## Page 49

Astronaut
Count by 2s to draw the astronaut.
Draw your face inside the astronaut's helmet.
The Never-Bored Kid Book • EMC 6304 • © Evan-Moor Corp.
49

## Page 50

Back to the Ship
Draw a line to help the astronaut get back to the ship.
50
The Never-Bored Kid Book • EMC 6304 • © Evan-Moor Corp.

## Page 52

Our Solar System
Mercury
Venus
Earth
Mars
52
The Never-Bored Kid Book • EMC 6304 • © Evan-Moor Corp.

## Page 53

Jupiter
Uranus
Neptune
Saturn
The Never-Bored Kid Book • EMC 6304 • © Evan-Moor Corp.
53

## Page 58

Name the Astronaut
Use the code to help you answer the riddles.
1—A 4—G 7—M 10—R 13—Y
2—D 5—I 8—N 11—S
3—E 6—L 9—O 12—T
Who was the first American woman in space?
SALLY RIDE
Who was the first man to set foot on the moon?
NEIL
ARMSTRONG
58
The Never-Bored Kid Book • EMC 6304 • © Evan-Moor Corp.

## Page 59

Voyager
Voyager is a space probe. It is one way scientists have explored the planets. Count by 2s to connect the dots to see Voyager.
The Never-Bored Kid Book • EMC 6304 • © Evan-Moor Corp.
59

## Page 60

Space Aliens
Find the space aliens hiding on the moon. Color them.
How many aliens did you find? 13
60
The Never-Bored Kid Book • EMC 6304 • © Evan-Moor Corp.

## Page 61

In the Rainforest
Find these rainforest animals in the word search.
Sloth
Boa Constrictor
Jaguar
Toucan
Anteater
Tapir
Bat
Poison Dart Frog
Howler Monkey
Can you find these rainforest plants? banana fig orchid
The Never-Bored Kid Book • EMC 6304 • © Evan-Moor Corp.
61

## Page 62

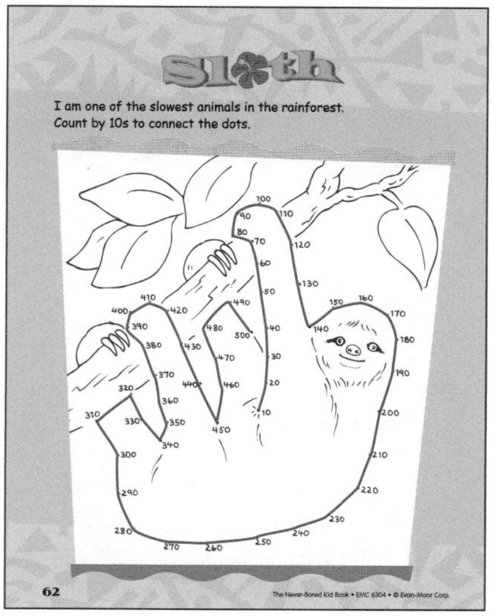
Sloth
I am one of the slowest animals in the rainforest. Count by 10s to connect the dots.
62
The Never-Bored Kid Book • EMC 6304 • © Evan-Moor Corp.

## Page 63

Rainforest Animals
Color the rainforest animals.
The Never-Bored Kid Book • EMC 6304 • © Evan-Moor Corp.
63

## Page 64

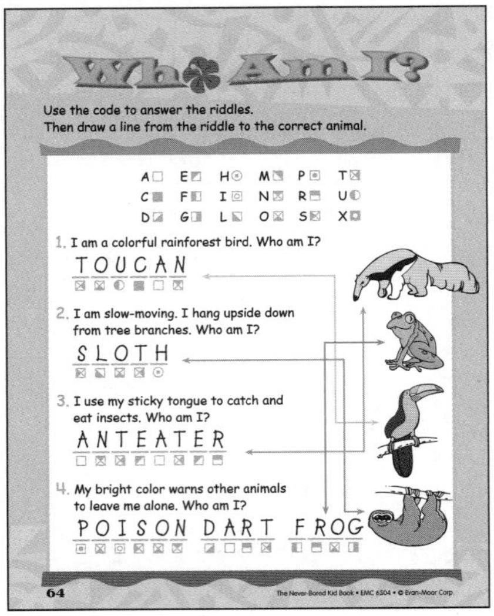
Who Am I?
Use the code to answer the riddles.
Then draw a line from the riddle to the correct animal.
1. I am a colorful rainforest bird. Who am I?
TOUCAN
2. I am slow-moving. I hang upside down from tree branches. Who am I?
SLOTH
3. I use my sticky tongue to catch and eat insects. Who am I?
ANTEATER
4. My bright color warns other animals to leave me alone. Who am I?
POISON DART FROG
64
The Never-Bored Kid Book • EMC 6304 • © Evan-Moor Corp.

## Page 65

Leaf-Cutter Ant
Draw a line to guide the leaf-cutter ant back to its nest.
START
END
The Never-Bored Kid Book • EMC 6304 • © Evan-Moor Corp.
65

## Page 67

A toucan lives in the rainforest. It is a very large bird.
It has a huge beak. Fruit is a toucan's favorite food.
It also eats bird eggs, insects, and tree frogs.
The Never-Bored Kid Book • EMC 6304 • © Evan-Moor Corp.
67

## Page 73

Treasure Map
POISON POND
SILVER SEA
MISERY MOUNTAIN
RAGING RIVER
SKULL ROCK
N
W
E
S
PALM TREE GROVE
The Never-Bored Kid Book • EMC 6304 • © Evan-Moor Corp.
73

## Page 74

All Aboard!
Start at 1. Connect the dots. Color the picture.
Blackbeard and his pirate crew are sailing off after treasure.
What do you think they will find?
Answers will vary.
74
The Never-Bored Kid Book • EMC 6304 • © Evan-Moor Corp.

## Page 75

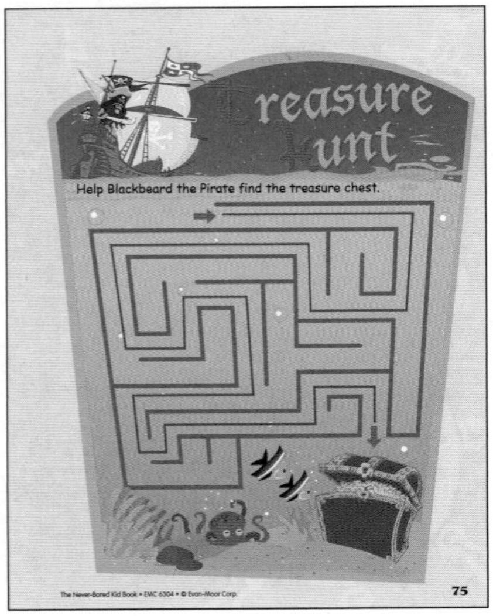
Treasure Hunt
Help Blackbeard the Pirate find the treasure chest.
The Never-Bored Kid Book • EMC 6304 • © Evan-Moor Corp.
75

## Page 77

How do you think Peg-Leg Pete lost his leg?
Answers will vary.
The Never-Bored Kid Book • EMC 6304 • © Evan-Moor Corp.
77

## Page 78

Pirates
Find the hidden words.
Word Box
anchor
captain
cannon
crew
crossbones
dagger
doubloons
gold
jewel
map
pirate
ship
silver
sword
treasure chest
78
The Never-Bored Kid Book • EMC 6304 • © Evan-Moor Corp.

## Page 79

Skull and Crossbones
When you see this flying over a ship, look out!
Start at 1. Connect the dots. Color the picture.
The Never-Bored Kid Book • EMC 6304 • © Evan-Moor Corp.
79

## Page 80

Name the Pirates
Use the code to name the pirates.
Captain Hook
Blackbeard
Captain Kidd
80
The Never-Bored Kid Book • EMC 6304 • © Evan-Moor Corp.

## Page 86

Making Popcorn
Cut out page 87. Glue the steps in order.
1 Get the popcorn from the cupboard.
2 Pour kernels into the popcorn popper.
3 Start the popper.
4 Wait for the kernels to pop.
5 Pour melted butter and salt on the popped corn.
6 Eat the popcorn.
86
The Never-Bored Kid Book • EMC 6304 • © Evan-Moor Corp.

## Page 89

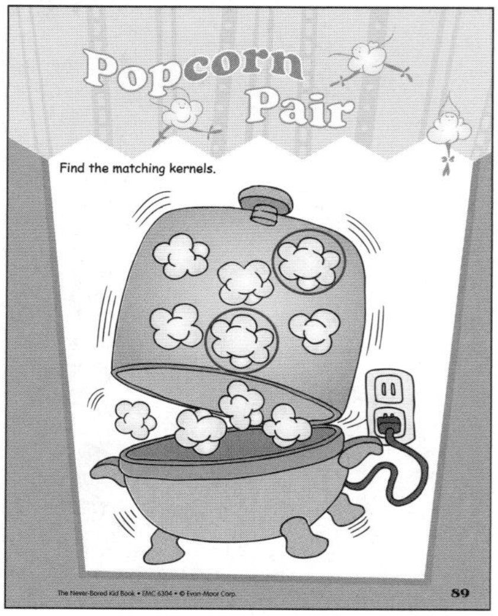
Popcorn Pair
Find the matching kernels.
The Never-Bored Kid Book • EMC 6304 • © Evan-Moor Corp.
89

## Page 90

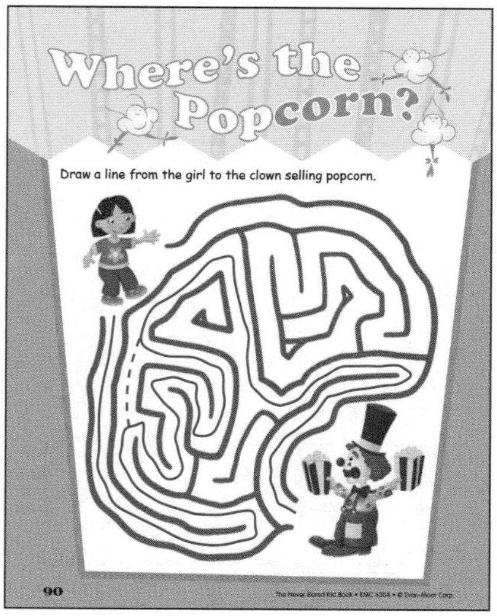
Where's the Popcorn?
Draw a line from the girl to the clown selling popcorn.
90
The Never-Bored Kid Book • EMC 6304 • © Evan-Moor Corp.

## Page 95

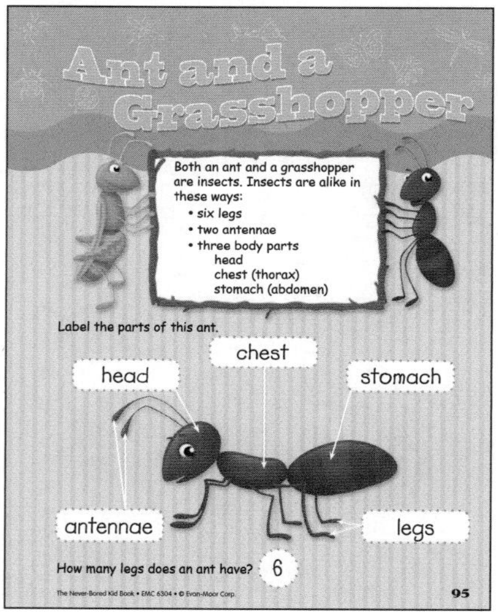
Ant and a Grasshopper
Both an ant and a grasshopper are insects. Insects are alike in these ways:
• six legs
• two antennae
• three body parts
head
chest (thorax)
stomach (abdomen)
Label the parts of this ant.
head
chest
stomach
antennae
legs
How many legs does an ant have? 6
The Never-Bored Kid Book • EMC 6304 • © Evan-Moor Corp.
95

## Page 103

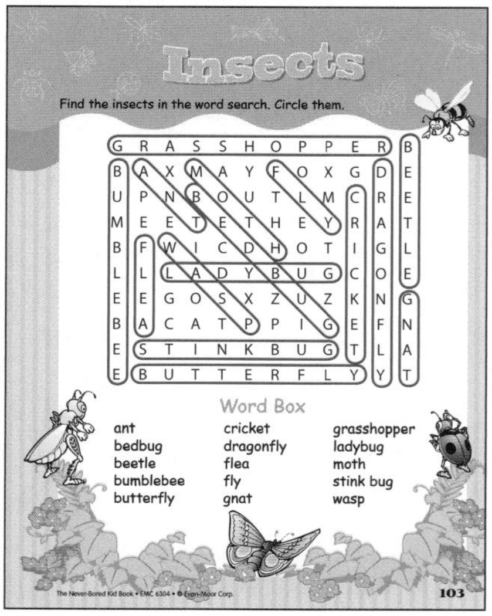
Insects
Find the insects in the word search. Circle them.
Word Box
ant
bedbug
beetle
bumblebee
butterfly
cricket
dragonfly
flea
fly
gnat
grasshopper
ladybug
moth
stink bug
wasp
The Never-Bored Kid Book • EMC 6304 • © Evan-Moor Corp.
103

## Page 104

Who Am I?
Use the code to name the insects.
Then draw a line from each name to the insect.
1. PRAYING MANTIS
2. LADYBIRD BEETLE
3. BUMBLEBEE
4. KATYDID
104
The Never-Bored Kid Book • EMC 6304 • © Evan-Moor Corp.

## Page 109

Stag Beetle
Draw and color the other side of this stag beetle.
The Never-Bored Kid Book • EMC 6304 • © Evan-Moor Corp.
109

## Page 110

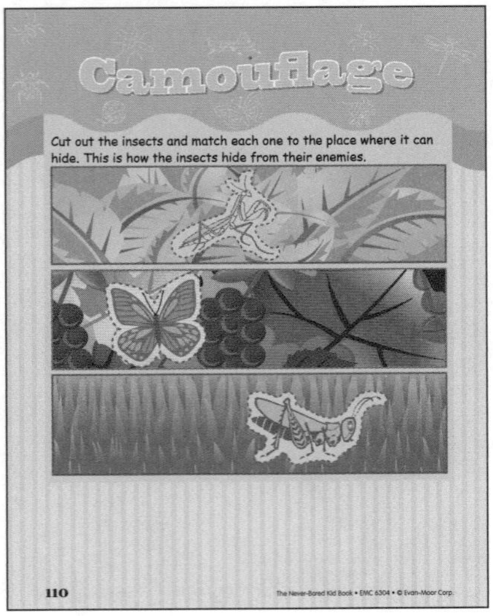
Camouflage
Cut out the insects and match each one to the place where it can hide. This is how the insects hide from their enemies.
110
The Never-Bored Kid Book • EMC 6304 • © Evan-Moor Corp.

## Page 111

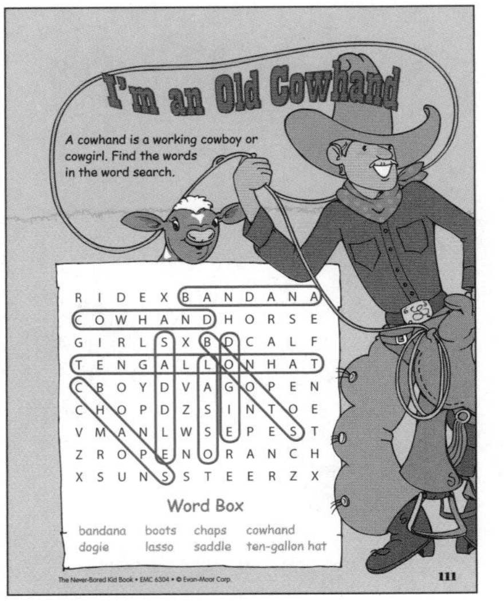
I'm an Old Cowhand
A cowhand is a working cowboy or cowgirl. Find the words in the word search.
R I D E X B A N D A N A
C O W H A N D H O R S E
G I R L S X B D C A L F
T E N G A L L O N H A T
C B O Y D V A G O P E N
C H O P D Z S I N T O E
V M A N L W S E P E S T
Z R O P E N O R A N C H
X S U N S S T E E R Z X
Word Box
bandana boots chaps cowhand
dogie lasso saddle ten-gallon hat
The Never-Bored Kid Book • EMC 6304 • © Evan-Moor Corp.
111

## Page 114

Herd of Cattle
Help the cowhand find the two cows that are exactly alike. Circle them.
Moo
Moo
Moo
Moo
Moo
Moo
Moo
114
The Never-Bored Kid Book • EMC 6304 • © Evan-Moor Corp.

## Page 115

My Horse
Read the clues. Circle my horse.
My horse has a white mark on his face.
My horse has spots.
My horse is black and white.
My horse has a black mane and tail.
Can you find him?
The Never-Bored Kid Book • EMC 6304 • © Evan-Moor Corp.
115

## Page 116

What Is It?
Start at 1. Connect the dots to find the mystery animal. Color it.
116
The Never-Bored Kid Book • EMC 6304 • © Evan-Moor Corp.

## Page 117

Little Lost Dogie
A dogie is a calf without a mother.
Help the cowhand find the lost dogie.
The Never-Bored Kid Book • EMC 6304 • © Evan-Moor Corp.
117

## Page 118

Ride 'em, Cowboy!
Cut out the puzzle pieces on page 119.
Glue them together here.
118
The Never-Bored Kid Book • EMC 6304 • © Evan-Moor Corp.

## Page 121

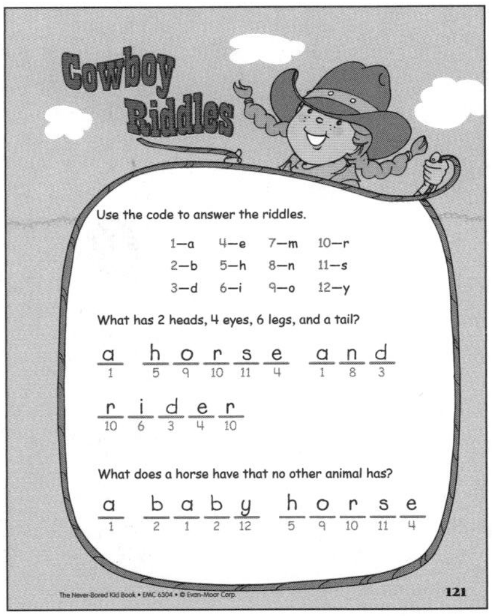
Cowboy Riddles
Use the code to answer the riddles.
1—a 4—e 7—m 10—r
2—b 5—h 8—n 11—s
3—d 6—i 9—o 12—y
What has 2 heads, 4 eyes, 6 legs, and a tail?
a horse and rider
What does a horse have that no other animal has?
a baby horse
The Never-Bored Kid Book • EMC 6304 • © Evan-Moor Corp.
121

## Page 127

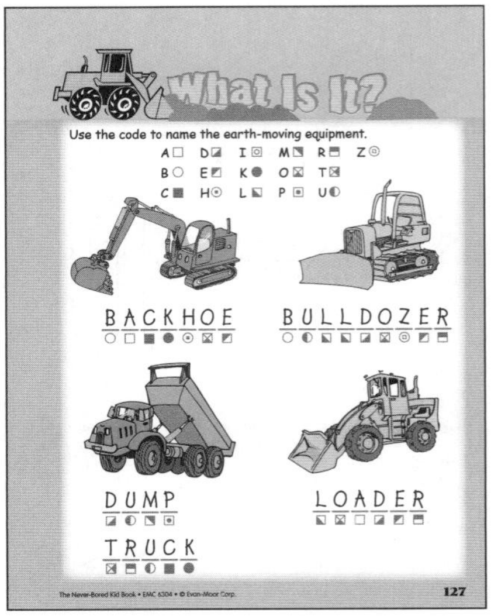
What Is It?
Use the code to name the earth-moving equipment.
BACKHOE
BULLDOZER
DUMP
LOADER
TRUCK
The Never-Bored Kid Book • EMC 6304 • © Evan-Moor Corp.
127

## Page 128

# Moving Dirt

Fill in the missing word to name the piece of equipment you would use to move the dirt.

I need to move a load of dirt to a new location.
I will use the dump truck.

I need to dig a trench for a new pipeline.
I will use the backhoe.

I need to lift dirt into the truck.
I will use the loader.

I need to move dirt into a pile.
I will use the bulldozer.

Word Box
bulldozer
loader
dump truck
backhoe

128 The Never-Bored Kid Book • EMC 6304 • © Evan-Moor Corp.

## Page 129

# Heavy Equipment

Circle what is wrong in this picture.


THIS SIDE UP


The Never-Bored Kid Book • EMC 6304 • © Evan-Moor Corp. 129

## Page 130

# Backhoe

Start at 2. Count by 2s. Connect the dots.

130 The Never-Bored Kid Book • EMC 6304 • © Evan-Moor Corp.

## Page 133

# Flightless Birds

Find these flightless birds in the word search.

| | | | | | | | | | |
|---|---|---|---|---|---|---|---|---|---|
| L | K | W | P | E | N | G | U | I | N |
| E | B | I | G | Z | M | X | F | A | R |
| G | N | U | W | O | D | U | C | K | A |
| O | S | T | R | I | C | H | T | E | N |
| O | C | A | S | S | O | W | A | R | Y |
| S | W | I | M | K | A | K | A | P | O |


kiwi
kakapo
ostrich
cassowary
emu
penguin


The Never-Bored Kid Book • EMC 6304 • © Evan-Moor Corp. 133

## Page 134

# What Am I?

Start at 2. Count by 2s to connect the dots. Color the picture.

Circle the name of the bird you made.

penguin ostrich kiwi

134 The Never-Bored Kid Book • EMC 6304 • © Evan-Moor Corp.

## Page 137

Penguins are flightless seabirds. They use their wings underwater as powerful flippers. Their bodies are covered by three layers of short feathers to keep them warm. These birds eat mostly fish and squid.

The Never-Bored Kid Book • EMC 6304 • © Evan-Moor Corp. 137

## Page 138

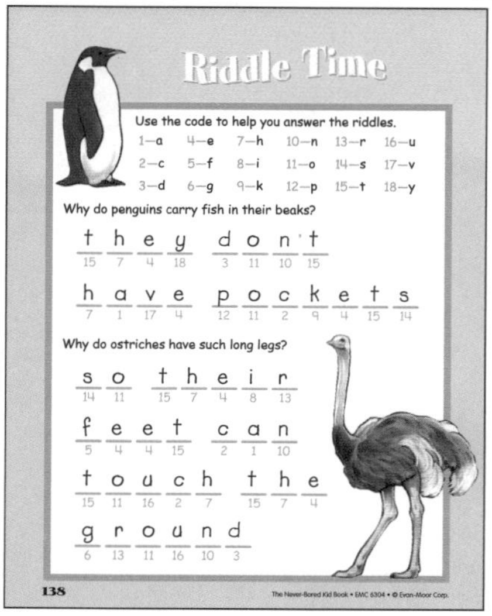

# Riddle Time

Use the code to help you answer the riddles.

| | | | | | |
|---|---|---|---|---|---|
| 1—a | 4—e | 7—h | 10—n | 13—r | 16—u |
| 2—c | 5—f | 8—i | 11—o | 14—s | 17—v |
| 3—d | 6—g | 9—k | 12—p | 15—t | 18—y |

Why do penguins carry fish in their beaks?

they don't
15 7 4 18 3 11 10 15

have pockets
7 1 17 4 12 11 2 9 4 15 14

Why do ostriches have such long legs?

so their
14 11 15 7 4 8 13

feet can
5 4 4 15 2 1 10

touch the
15 11 16 2 7 15 7 4

ground
6 13 11 16 10 3

138 The Never-Bored Kid Book • EMC 6304 • © Evan-Moor Corp.

## Page 139

# Where Are My Babies?

Mother Ostrich has lost her babies. She needs your help to find them. Color the babies as you find them in this picture.

How many babies did you find in all? 8

The Never-Bored Kid Book • EMC 6304 • © Evan-Moor Corp. 139

## Page 140

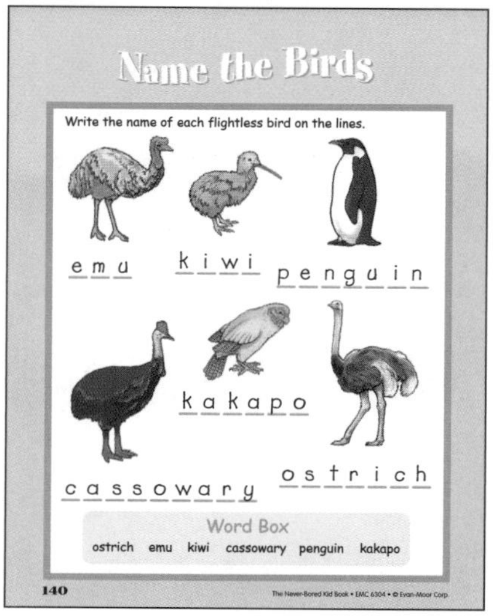

# Name the Birds

Write the name of each flightless bird on the lines.

emu kiwi penguin

kakapo

cassowary ostrich

Word Box
ostrich emu kiwi cassowary penguin kakapo

140 The Never-Bored Kid Book • EMC 6304 • © Evan-Moor Corp.

## Page 141

Bread Search
How many times can you find bread in the puzzle? 6
J A M B R E A D M I L K
B R E A D B T N A A N B
Z L O A F R O B T P C R
R O S L I E R I Z P R E
Y B A G L A T N O L A A
E P I T A D I G E S C D
B R E A D S L I C E K X
M U F F I N L B A G E L
S U N B R E A D O O R D
Now find these kinds of bread.
bagel matzo roll loaf
bun naan rye muffin
cracker pita slice tortilla
The Never-Bored Kid Book • EMC 6304 • © Evan-Moor Corp.
141

## Page 142

All Kinds of Bread
Cut out the puzzle pieces on page 143.
Glue them together here.
142
The Never-Bored Kid Book • EMC 6304 • © Evan-Moor Corp.

## Page 145

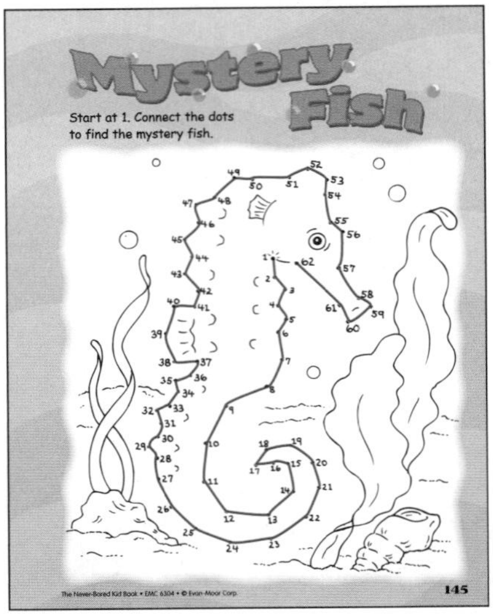
Mystery Fish
Start at 1. Connect the dots
to find the mystery fish.
The Never-Bored Kid Book • EMC 6304 • © Evan-Moor Corp.
145

## Page 147

Name the Parts
coronet
eye
snout
body
dorsal fin
tail
Look at the picture. Then do the crossword puzzle.
Across
3. the largest part of a sea horse
5. this part moves the sea horse around
6. this part is used for seeing
Down
1. the top of the sea horse's head
2. this part can curl around sea grass
4. the nose and mouth part of a sea horse
The Never-Bored Kid Book • EMC 6304 • © Evan-Moor Corp.
147

## Page 151

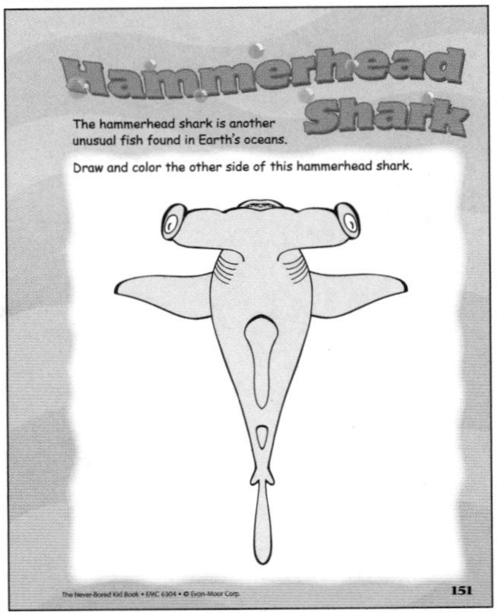
Hammerhead Shark
The hammerhead shark is another unusual fish found in Earth's oceans.
Draw and color the other side of this hammerhead shark.
The Never-Bored Kid Book • EMC 6304 • © Evan-Moor Corp.
151